Noah Miller Ludlow.
Courtesy of the Theatre Collection,
New York Public Library.

THE THEATRE IN EARLY KENTUCKY

WEST T. HILL, Jr.

The Theatre in Early Kentucky

1790-1820

THE UNIVERSITY PRESS OF KENTUCKY

Standard Book Number 8131-1240-0
Library of Congress Catalog Card Number 73-132829

Copyright © 1971 BY THE UNIVERSITY PRESS OF KENTUCKY

A statewide cooperative scholarly publishing agency serving Berea College,
Centre College of Kentucky, Eastern Kentucky University, Kentucky State
College, Morehead State University, Murray State University, University of
Kentucky, University of Louisville, and Western Kentucky University.
Editorial and Sales Offices: Lexington, Kentucky 40506

For Dorothy Belle

Contents

Illustrations

Preface

THIS is a chronological record of theatrical production in the area of America's first frontier, beginning with the earliest stage announcement in 1790 and concluding with Samuel Drake's established Kentucky Circuit in 1819. These twenty-nine years represent a distinct period in American theatre, the struggle to establish dramatic production in what had only recently been the domain of the Indians and the long gun hunters. After 1820 dramatic art witnessed a widespread growth. Traveling companies organized by Ludlow, Caldwell, Turner, Collins and Jones, Drake, and others moved into many areas of the West and South. The early pioneer era of western stage development was over.

Furthermore, this is a theatrical record, not a literary analysis or evaluation of the dramas of the period. I have in the main recorded information about theatres, methods of production, actors, managers, circuits, performances, and critical reviews. Theatrical notices in the early western newspapers were the principal source. Although these advertisements were at times fragmentary and sporadic, they constitute the most accurate production data for the period. To avoid routine listings of performance data in the text, I have included a complete production record in the appendix.

The earliest American stage historians recorded theatrical development in the populated centers: New York, Philadelphia, Boston, Baltimore, and Charleston. They paid little attention to the growing interests in drama production west of the Allegheny Mountains. Although stage activity, both amateur and professional, flourished in certain areas of that region after 1790, it was generally ignored by writers of theatrical history until the twentieth century.

A few actors and managers who worked the western circuits wrote memoirs, journals, and diary accounts of their activities in the theatre. The best of these, Noah Miller Ludlow's *Dramatic Life As I Found It*, was not published until 1880, sixty years after the early period. Nevertheless, throughout the twentieth century Ludlow's account of his experiences in the West and South has been the principal source of early western stage activity; in fact contemporary stage historians usually treat the frontier period with little more detail than a cursory quotation from his narrative of the Drakes' trek to Kentucky in 1815. Interesting and significant as Ludlow's journal is, it is not a history of the early western theatre, nor is it a record of early theatrical performances. Indeed theatrical activity had been developing, especially in Kentucky, for years before Ludlow arrived on the scene.

That Kentucky was the principal area of western drama production before 1820 is a matter of statistical record. Kentucky audiences witnessed nearly 600 dramatic performances from 1790 to 1820, an almost unbelievable number, especially compared with the dearth of theatrical production in other parts of the West during the same period. Cincinnati, the only town in Ohio that recorded performances during the same period, had 54; and St. Louis, representing Missouri, had 32.[1] Thus the record of stage activity in Kentucky before 1820 represents nearly a complete theatrical history of the American West during this early period. The pioneer dramatic development in Kentucky made significant contributions to later theatrical enterprises throughout the West and the South.

I wish to express my gratitude to those who have helped me at the University of Chicago Library Rare Books Department, the New York Public Library Theatre Collection, the Lincoln Center for the Performing Arts Library, the Library

---

[1] William G. B. Carson, *The Theatre on the Frontier: The Early Years of the St. Louis Stage* (Chicago, 1932), pp. 318-19. Hereafter cited as *The Theatre on the Frontier*.

of Congress Rare Books Division, the Kentucky Room of the Louisville Public Library, the Filson Club in Louisville, the Cincinnati Historical Society, the Missouri Historical Society, the University of Pittsburgh Library, the Lexington Public Library, and the Kentucky Historical Society in Frankfort. For help with particular aspects of the study I am grateful to Mrs. Dorothy Cullen, former curator of the Filson Club; the late Mr. G. Glenn Clift, assistant director and editor of the Kentucky Historical Society; and Mrs. Sabra Barbour, librarian of the Centre College of Kentucky Library. I wish to thank Mr. J. Winston Coleman, Jr., and the late Mr. Charles Staples, Kentucky historians, for their help with local historical and theatrical information. I am especially grateful to Dr. John J. Weisert, professor of modern languages at the University of Louisville, who kindly provided valuable newspaper materials and offered general assistance with some of the research. I should like to thank Mr. William G. B. Carson and the publishing company of Benjamin Blom for permission to use the picture of Julia Dean, the publishers Harper and Brothers for permission to use the picture of "Jim Crow" Rice, and Mr. Charles A. Thomas of Danville, Kentucky, for providing most of the photographs taken from early newspapers. Finally, I am grateful to Centre College, which provided financial aid for this research.

* 1 *

The Athens of the West

KENTUCKY, the "dark and bloody ground," became a melting pot for many American pioneers after their struggle for independence. Restless people from southern coastal cities arrived in the Kentucky wilderness through the Cumberland Gap and the Wilderness Road. From Pittsburgh and other northern river settlements others floated down the Ohio River to a bustling northern Kentucky landing called Limestone, now Maysville. Settlers crowding these two routes converged in Kentucky and to their surprise found the thriving town of Lexington, which was such a contrast to the rugged surrounding wilderness that they called it "the Athens of the West."

Lexington, established as a permanent settlement in 1779, supported in 1787 the first western newspaper, the *Kentucke Gazette*. In 1798 Transylvania University, the first university west of the Alleghenies, opened with "a group of well-trained scholars and students drawn from a wide radius."[1] One theatrical historian, in describing Williamsburg, Virginia, as the right place for the beginning of colonial theatrical development, mentions the public buildings, the college, and the shops loaded with merchandise.[2] The same could be said for Lexington, for by 1800, with a population of 2,400,[3] it was the largest city in the West. At this time Lexington could boast not only of a newspaper and a university but also of a post office, twenty-four retail stores, and tobacco and whiskey export industries. The university, a union of the Kentucky Academy and Transylvania

1

Seminary, offered courses in such subjects as languages, natural philosophy, astronomy, mathematics, and geography. Both a medical and a law school served the students, who paid fifteen pounds a year for board, "paid half yearly in advance," and who furnished their own bedding, washing, wood, and candles.[4]

One traveler on a tour of the western country in 1806 described Lexington as having roads which "were very wide and fine, with grazing parks, meadows, and every spot in sight cultivated." He was impressed by the spacious streets (particularly the eighty-foot wide main street), the large brick houses, and the sidewalks. The courthouse, where many of the dramatic presentations were held, was a good, three-story brick building adorned with a cupola, a bell, and a clock. If this were not enough to draw the venturesome from the East, other Lexington attractions included a public library, three boarding schools for women, and several day schools for men, with one hundred pupils altogether.[5]

Like Williamsburg, this western community had the environment—the leisure, learning, and culture—necessary for theatre development. The real problem facing all the western settlements was transportation and communication. Travel between Lexington and eastern points was slow, difficult, and often dangerous. If a rutty, log-strewn clearing can be called a road, then the Cumberland Gap Road, completed in 1796, was the first road through the mountains. Settlers coming into Kentucky on this road from the southeast could haul as much as a ton of goods, providing they had four good horses. Advertisements in the *Kentucky Gazette* lured the more adventuresome over the mountains with assurances of abundant crops, road-

---

[1] Oral Sumner Coad and Edwin Mims, Jr., *The Pageant of America*, 15 vols. (New Haven, Conn., 1929), 14: 123.

[2] Arthur Hornblow, *A History of the Theatre in America*, 2 vols. (New York, 1919), 1: 39.

[3] George W. Ranck, *History of Lexington, Kentucky, Its Early Annals and Recent Progress* (Cincinnati, Ohio, 1872), p. 220.

[4] *Kentucky Gazette*, 2 January 1800. Hereafter cited as *Gazette*.

[5] Fortescue Cuming, *Sketches of a Tour to the Western Country, through the States of Ohio and Kentucky. . .*, vol. 4, *Early Western Travels, 1748–1846. . .*, ed. Reuben Gold Thwaites (Cleveland, Ohio, 1904), pp. 181-82, 184. Hereafter cited as *Sketches of a Tour to the Western Country*.

side necessities, minimum expenses, and other chamber-of-commerce-like enticements;[6] but the same newspaper announced daring Indian raids in and around Lexington as late as 1800. The other wagon road, from Limestone to Lexington, had been a thoroughfare since 1787, Limestone being the westernmost river landing during the early period. It was named "Smith's Wagon Road" after the man who first brought a wagon team from Limestone to Lexington.[7] Stagecoaches were operating in and around Lexington by 1803,[8] but steamboat service on the Ohio River did not reach St. Louis until 1817.[9] As late as 1815, Samuel Drake brought his theatrical troupe to Kentucky from New York by floating down the Allegheny and Ohio rivers on crude flat-bottomed boats. In 1816 he took two days to travel from Frankfort to Louisville, a distance of about fifty miles.[10] It is understandable that John Bernard, manager of the Boston Theatre, refused an invitation to manage the newly organized Lexington Theatre in 1808.[11]

For those who successfully made the trip over the mountains or down the river, the bustling town of Lexington teemed with trade and politics, amateur entertainment and culture. Not only did Lexington have amateur stage productions before 1800; there were also musical concerts, debates, sermons, dancing, and a variety of homespun amusements reflecting the character of the pioneer people. Furthermore, there were the strolling charlatans—acrobats, wire-walkers, magicians, fortune-tellers, gamblers, musicians, dancers—all the itinerant showmen who found their way over the mountains in pursuit of the gullible, fun-loving settler. This rabble of carnival folk always served as the forerunner to the professional actor, who was often a magician or a showman turned actor and who just as

[6] *Gazette,* 8 October 1796.
[7] J. Winston Coleman, Jr., *Stage-Coach Days in the Bluegrass* (Louisville, Ky., 1935), pp. 26-27.
[8] Lewis Collins, *History of Kentucky,* 2 vols. (Covington, Ky., 1882), 1: 514.
[9] Ralph Leslie Rusk, *The Literature of the Middle Western Frontier,* 2 vols. (New York, 1925), 1: 24.
[10] Noah Miller Ludlow, *Dramatic Life As I Found It* (New York, 1966) p. 88. Hereafter cited as *Dramatic Life.*
[11] John Bernard, *Retrospections of America, 1797–1811* (New York, 1887), p. 336. Hereafter cited as *Retrospections of America.*

often reverted to his cruder talents when the necessity arose. But most entertainment came from the citizens themselves, who formed thespian societies, musical societies, debating societies, and numerous literary and political clubs.

The innkeeper in Lexington, like the innkeeper in Elizabethan England, assumed the role of entrepreneur, master of ceremonies, and theatrical agent. By necessity, but often also by choice, he offered his guests a variety of amusements and a hall or other place of performance not only for dramatic presentations but also for local debates, musicals, and exhibitions of various kinds. That innkeeping in early Lexington was a lucrative business is revealed by the numerous quaint signs in the *Kentucky Gazette* advertising The Red Lion, The Sign of the Buffalo, The Sign of the Green Tree, The Eagle Tavern, and The Sign of the Ship. Luke Usher, the first theatrical promoter in the West, advertised his inn accommodations in rhyme in the *Gazette*, May 8, 1818:

Entertainment For Travellers

Who's not been in Kentucky hath not seen the world;
'Tis the state in which Freedom's own flag is unfurl'd!
It is plenty's headquarters—'tis Misery's grave;
Where the ladies are lovely, and Men are all brave!
When the weary and hungry to Lexington trip,
Let them stop and regale at the sign of *The Ship*,
Where I promise to treat them as well as I'm able,
With a larder well stor'd and good liquors, and stable:

Luke Usher,
Ship Inn, in Short Street
2 doors from Limestone
at Lexington.

Competition among innkeepers to see which could promote the best or at least the most unique entertainment prepared the way for theatrical activity in the area after 1800. In 1806 local musicians performed in Bradley's popular assembly room in Traveller's Hall Inn. Here Lexingtonians could listen to both vocal and instrumental music in a room that was "superbly illuminated and kept warm." The prices of admission were twenty-five and fifty cents. Proceeds from these performances went for "the relief of distressed humanity" (a worthy, if widespread, cause). Bradley's room, advertised as being located in the public square in the center of the business district, measured fifty-four by thirty-two feet and served as both assembly room and dining hall. The Lexington Debating Society met at the Coffee House in 1807 to debate the practice of "Physic" in Kentucky, one resolution of which would prohibit anyone to practice who had not taken "a regular course of study." A man named Nugent opened a dancing school in Bradley's room in 1805 and advertised for twenty pupils. Such dancing schools were popular in Lexington as early as 1788, when John Davenport advertised for both ladies and gentlemen to be taught at Captain Young's by the quarter. In 1789 Jeremiah Moriarty offered his services as a dancing instructor both in Lexington and in Danville; he also taught the use of globes, by the day or by the quarter, at five dollars per quarter. Students brought their own lunches. In 1801 the admirers of pulpit eloquence were invited to the store of McBean and Poyzer, where they could hear (if their applications were early) sermons on such lofty topics as "The Death of George Washington."[12] At the same time students at Transylvania University were pronouncing orations in the Presbyterian meetinghouse.[13]

Inns were not only the popular places for amusement and instruction in the early West; they served also as meetinghouses for more serious business. The town of Frankfort became the capital of Kentucky in 1792 at a meeting in Brent's Tavern in Lexington.[14] In 1795 a public library was established at McNair's Tavern, and on March 12, 1805, the trustees of Lexington met at Wilson's Tavern to hear claims on a property settlement.[15]

Not all the activities sponsored by the inn were cultural,

[12] *Gazette*, 8 March, 16 January 1806, 29 December 1807, 24 September 1805, 22 March 1788, 27 June 1789, 14 September 1801.
[13] *Lexington Reporter*, 26 September 1808. Hereafter cited as *Reporter*.
[14] Coleman, *Stage-Coach Days*, p. 63.
[15] *Gazette*, 10 January 1795, 12 March 1805.

instructional, or political. The innkeepers advertised a steady fare of more spectacular entertainments for those not interested in music or debating. At Postlethwait's Inn the citizens had an opportunity to see "The Siamese Twin Brothers." Candy's Tavern advertised "The Gigantic Giraffe," and "An African Lion" was displayed at Satterwhite's Inn. One of the most popular forms of dramatic display, which swept the country during the eighteenth and early nineteenth centuries, was the wax figure exhibition. The Kentucky Hotel in Lexington advertised in 1809 an exhibition of wax figures representing such renowned historical figures as President Washington, Napoleon, Alexander Hamilton, Aaron Burr, and General Braddock.[16] These wax figures were the first dramatic tableaux that many pioneer settlers had ever seen. One strolling actor performing before a rural audience overheard a spectator say that the performers in a particular scene were not wax figures since there were no strings attached.[17] Apparently wax figures were not only displayed motionless but were also manipulated by strings like puppets.

The inn was by no means the only source of diversion for Lexington citizens. Animal fighting, bearbaiting, horseracing, gambling, and other activities, both indoors and out, helped the westerner pass his leisure hours. Just as the innyard had its influence on the construction of Elizabethan theatres, so did the bearbaiting and cockfighting pits. The gory particulars of bearbaiting in Kentucky at the beginning of the nineteenth century speak for themselves in a description in J. Winston Coleman's *Stage-Coach Days in the Bluegrass:*

"Rare Sport

"To the lovers of Sport, their attention is called that on the 29th of December there will be a

"Bear Baiting

"At my house on the Cynthiana Road, one mile from Paris at 10 o'clock A.M. when a three year old HE BEAR will be turned

[16] Ibid., 11 June 1805, 29 August 1809.
[17] *Dramatic Life,* p. 12.

loose and five dogs will be entered every half hour to fight him; according to regulations to be made known at the time of entering.

"ALSO, the half of a SHE BEAR will be barbecued and as good a dinner furnished as the country can provide. No quarrelsome person will be permitted to remain as guest as peace and harmony will be promoted and expected.

"O. A. FORSYTHE[18]

There was no end to the array of spectacular feats, displays of magic, and exhibitions of animals. Where the performers came from or how they made their way to this western settlement remains a mystery, but here they were. In 1805 a man named Rannie exhibited at Traveller's Hall a series of magical deceptions: he broke watches, both gold and silver (no mention is made of the results of this experiment), made watches move mysteriously across the floor, performed surgical operations without pain, swallowed knives, beheaded chickens (and restored them), caught bullets fired from a pistol, and threw his voice. Moreover, he was an actor in regular drama and often performed feats of magic as an added attraction to the stage piece. A man named Church, performing at the Kentucky Hotel, imitated the calls of the redbird, the robin, and the chicken; he also did a balancing act on a slack wire and danced blindfolded over thirteen eggs. A man named Bury held a display of animals, one of which, "the Cassowara of India," weighed 150 pounds; also included in this exhibition were Barbary apes. If this were not enough, there was music on the violin, organ, and clarinet between the displays.[19] The renowned Gaston produced displays of fireworks and an ascent of a balloon sixty feet in circumference—all announced by the firing of a cannon in Robert Barr's lot.

Horseracing, Kentucky's "sport of kings," commanded a following in Lexington as early as 1787, possibly earlier. One announcement in the *Gazette* of August 29, 1789, called attention to a purse race at Lexington which was free to any

[18] Coleman, *Stage-Coach Days*, pp. 60-61
[19] *Gazette*, 30 April 1805, 31 October 1814.

horse, mare, or gelding. The distance was a three-mile heat; the owners paid a one-guinea fee, and the judges were selected by the majority of starters. Open gambling, however, was frowned upon by the local authorities. On March 12, 1805, according to the *Gazette* of the same day, a number of citizens went with the magistrates and the sheriff to a house where a gambling table was in operation; they seized it and burned it in the courthouse yard.

One could truly say of Lexington, as Hornblow had said of Williamsburg, "It was just the place to support a theatre." The wax figures and the charlatans made ways for the "live" actors, the people who recited lines, laughed, fought, and died on the stage. These real actors, few in number at first, made their way across the mountains and down the river, acting in barns, courthouses, and inns. They were not the Keans, the Garricks, or the Kembles; but to the eyes of the pioneer audiences they were just as good, for few, if any, of these spectators had ever seen Kean, Garrick, or Kemble perform.

* 2 *

The First Dramatic Performances

O N April 26, 1790, an interesting theatrical review in the *Kentucky Gazette* announced the performance on April 10 of an unnamed tragedy and farce by the students of Transylvania Seminary "in the presence of a very respectable audience." It was the first announced dramatic performance west of the Allegheny Mountains. A fragment of a notice in a damaged issue of the *Pittsburgh Gazette*, April 17, 1790, advertised a performance of Rowe's tragedy *Cato* and Isaac Jackman's farce *All the World's a Stage*, but the date, place of performance, and other production information are lost in the missing section of the announcement.[1] These ambitious programs show that audiences were accustomed to lengthy dramatic entertainments. Theatrical programs also offered much variety, and seldom did a performing group produce only one piece for an evening of entertainment. The Transylvania students and the Pittsburgh players were simply following traditional stage practices.

No other theatrical announcement appeared in any western journal until seven years after the Transylvania performance. On September 30, 1797, the *Washington* (Kentucky) *Mirror*, a weekly, printed a notice of a performance by the "Theatrical Society" to be acted in the "Court House" on Thursday evening, October 12. The notice (erroneously dated September 29, 1796) announced the performance of *Douglas, Love-a-la-Mode*, and *The Padlock*; the admission price was "Half-a-dollar," and members of the audience were forbidden to enter behind the scenes. This is the first record of a western stage performance to reveal play titles, date of production, place, and other significant information.

It may seem surprising that Washington, Kentucky, then a village of a few hundred people, could stage one of the first identifiable dramatic performances in the West; but it was one of the oldest settlements in the state and the seat of Mason County until 1848, when Maysville assumed that office. At the time of the production Washington had about 500 inhabitants.[2] Anthony Philip Heinrich, a musician traveling in Kentucky in 1817, described Washington as a "considerable village, . . . a town laid out on a large scale in the heart of a very fertile valley."[3]

The title "Theatrical Society" used by the Washington group was one of the many names chosen by amateur stage organizations during the early period. After 1800 strolling players in Kentucky found organized stage activity sponsored by groups named "the Thespians" and "the Roscians." Various amateur groups had developed drama production in Kentucky for years before the first strolling professional was advertised in 1810, and amateurs performed with professionals for a number of years after 1810.

Following the tradition of professional productions during the period, the Washington amateurs presented an ambitious program. Of course, the plays were the popular stock pieces of the day, but even so, it must have been no small task to bring this variety of drama and music to the boards.

The three pieces announced by the Theatrical Society had been extremely popular in Great Britain throughout the latter part of the eighteenth century and remained popular for years afterward. *Douglas, or The Noble Shepherd*, by the Reverend

[1] Alfred McClung Lee, "Trends in Commercial Entertainment in Pittsburgh As Reflected in the Advertising in Pittsburgh's Newspapers (1790-1860)" (master's thesis, University of Pittsburgh, 1931), p. 117. Hereafter cited as "Trends in Commercial Entertainment."

[2] W. H. Perrin et al., *Kentucky: A History of the State* (Louisville, Ky., 1887), p. 705.

[3] William Treat Upton, *Anthony Philip Heinrich* (New York, 1939), p. 27.

John Home was the rave of the century. It was a classic of the poetic-romantic, melodramatic style of writing. *Douglas,* a sentimental tale taken from an old Scottish ballad, tells the story of a lost child, reared by a shepherd, who is revealed to be Young Norval, the son of Lady Randolph who was formerly Lady Douglas. The young man saves the life of Lord Randolph only to be killed later by him. Lady Randolph, learning of her son's death, kills herself.

The author, criticized by the ruling body of his church for his exploits into the theatrical world, was summoned before the Presbytery but resigned his position before the proceeding could be carried out.[4] *Douglas* was performed successfully in Edinburgh in 1756 before a crowded house. Home, seated in the audience, proudly heard one Scotsman yell, "Whaur's yer Wully Shakespeare noo!"[5]

Although the renowned Samuel Johnson could not find ten good lines in *Douglas,* there were others who considered it the outstanding dramatic piece of the century. The poet Thomas Gray felt that *Douglas* had recaptured "the true language of the stage, which had been lost for two hundred years." The great David Garrick made the mistake of his career in refusing to act the part of Young Norval, fearing that Mrs. Cibber, in the role of Lady Randolph, would outshine him. Handsome Spranger Barry took the role and was an overnight success.[6]

For years afterward schoolchildren memorized the opening lines of Young Norval, the Stranger: "My name is Norval; on the Grampion hills my father feeds his flock, a frugal swain." Although the play is not performed today, it moved the emotions of Kentucky audiences, some of whom had never seen actors on a stage.

The second offering by the amateurs of Washington was *Love-a-la-Mode, or The Humor of the Turf,* a two-act satirical farce by Charles Macklin, the celebrated English actor. It

4 *DNB,* 9: 1130.
5 Phyllis Hartnoll, *The Oxford Companion to the Theatre* (London, 1951), p. 370. Hereafter cited as *Oxford Companion.*
6 *DNB,* 1: 1130.

was first produced at Drury Lane in 1760. Like many actors of the period, Macklin dabbled in playwriting; this was one of his better pieces. (As an actor he was best known for rescuing Shakespeare's Shylock from the crudities of the low comic type; in Macklin's hands Shylock for the first time assumed a serious character.) *Love-a-la-Mode*, famous for its comic characters Sir Archy MacSarcasm and Sir Callaghan O'Brallaghan, was one of the most popular farcial afterpieces of the period. The farce concerns four suitors who are rivals for the hand of a lady; an Irishman (originally played by Macklin), an Englishman, a Scotsman, and a Jew. The lady pretends to lose her fortune in order to discover which of the four is her sincere lover.

If this low comic plot did not please the Washington audience, there was still more to follow—a musical piece by Isaac Bickerstaffe, *The Padlock*. Charles Dibdin, a prolific writer of musical plays in England during the eighteenth century, not only wrote the music for this one but also played the leading role, Mungo, in the original production in 1769. Bickerstaffe based the story on *The Jealous Husband*, a novel by Cervantes. The preposterous plot of *The Padlock* centers on Diego, guardian of Leonora, his bride-to-be. He padlocks her door, but young Leander, Leonora's lover, gains admission with the help of a comic character, Mungo. Diego, fearing the worst, sings:

> My door shall be lock'd,
> My windows be block'd;
> No male in my house,
> Not so much as a mouse;
> Then horns, horns, I defy you.

The character Mungo, considered by many to be the first stage Negro, was originally written for John Moody, an actor who studied the dialects and manners of West Indian Negroes. Lewis Hallam, Jr., first played the role in America in 1769 at the John Street Theatre in New York. He was so convincing in the role and became so associated with it that the character was seldom portrayed by any other actor. At one place in the musical, Mungo sings a pathetic song concerning his existence:

> Dear heart, what a terrible life I am led!
> A dog has a better that's sheltered and fed.
> Night and day 'tis the same;
> My pain is deir game;
> Me wish to de Lord me was dead!
> Whate'er's to be done
> Pore black man must run.
> Mungo here, Mungo dere,
> Mungo everywhere;
> Above and below,
> Sirrah, come, sirrah, go;
> Do so, and do so.
> Oh! Oh!
> Me wish to de Lord me was dead![7]

The purpose of this rather detailed analysis of the three dramas performed in Washington, Kentucky, in 1797, is to show just what kind of drama the area was destined to witness for the next twenty-five years. Had the Washington *Mirror* announced Shakespeare's *Hamlet* or Sheridan's *The Rivals*, no analysis would have been necessary; but who has heard of *The Padlock* or *Love-a-la-Mode?* Yet these were two of the most popular pieces of their kind in the eighteenth and early nineteenth centuries, both in England and in America.

Though the seventeenth century in England, beginning with Shakespeare and ending with Congreve, was one of the world's richest periods in dramatic literature, the next century produced little English drama of literary merit. This statement must not be misconstrued to mean that the eighteenth century was not an outstanding period of acting, managing, and theatre production. Dramatists were more numerous than ever before, and plays of every description came from their pens almost faster than they could be produced. One need only glance at the roster of actors and actor-managers such as Cibber, Rich,

[7] Laurence Hutton, *Curiosities of the American Stage* (New York, 1891), pp. 93-94.

Garrick, and Macklin to see that the plays, bad as many of them were, became popular acting vehicles for these stars, who performed them repeatedly to receptive audiences. It was an outstanding period of theatre but an abysmally poor age of drama. Comedy had lost its seventeenth-century wit in favor of sentimental triviality, and tragedy had degenerated into romantic melodrama, domestic sentiment, and spectacular intrigue. Few of the writers are known today and seldom are their plays performed. There are a few exceptions: Richard Brinsley Sheridan briefly revived the comedy of manners; Oliver Goldsmith, George Farquhar, and John Gay, with a delightful comedy of intrigue and farcial mixup, injected a fresh breath into a rather stale atmosphere. Gay's *Beggar's Opera* made the musical play such a popular form that by the end of the eighteenth century musical pieces had become standard offerings with tragedy and comedy.

No theatre program at this time was complete unless it offered a serious play or a comedy, followed by a farce or a musical piece, sometimes both. Often a pantomime concluded the program. In addition to all this the actors sang, danced, or recited between the plays or at the end. The theatre program in Washington, with its tragedy, farce, and musical piece, followed the theatrical practice of the time. Since audiences expected this variety of entertainment in one evening, the managers obliged and the writers turned out hundreds of comedies, farces, afterpieces, musicals, and pantomimes. Many were silly, trite, and poorly written, but they were popular. Macklin's *Love-a-la-Mode*, unknown today, always drew a good house, especially when Macklin played Sir Archy MacSarcasm. This farce and others like it survived well into the nineteenth century.

Needless to say, acting during this period required versatility, especially from those who undertook pioneering ventures in the new country. Mrs. Anne Hartley Gilbert, an actress of a later period in Kentucky, related that audiences first witnessed a serious piece, then a dance or a dance with song, then a farce or perhaps several farces; she would often perform in all the farces and dance in between them.[8] Samuel Drake, Jr., who acted in his father's pioneer company in Kentucky as early as 1815, frequently undertook more than one role in a play. After being killed in the last act of one of the pieces, he was required to fall far enough offstage to be able to play slow music on his violin as the curtain closed.[9]

Four months before the Washington production an article appeared in the *Gazette* of May 31, 1797, describing a new exhibition hall built on a lot in Lexington belonging to a man named Saunders, situated next to Coleman's Tavern. Although the article does not mention any play performed in this building, it was the first advertised structure in the West having all the physical characteristics of a theatre of the period, namely, a pit and a gallery. No mention is made of the stage, but there must have been one to accommodate the variety of feats advertised: wire-dancing, balancing acts, and tumbling. (Besides, it is unlikely that the builder would have erected a pit and a gallery without including a stage.) Admittance to the pit cost three shillings, ninepence; the gallery seats were two shillings, threepence.

Two years after the notice about the exhibition room the *Gazette* announced the performance of three different programs of plays, two in March and one in November of 1799. On February 28, 1799, the newspaper advertised two productions, one for March 5 and one "ON FRIDAY EVENING NEXT." This presentation on Friday, March 1, 1799, sponsored by the students of Transylvania University, included *The Busy Body* by Susannah Centlivre and the old favorite, *Love-a-la-Mode.* An unnamed group performing in the courthouse announced the offering for March 5: *He Would Be a Soldier* by Frederick Pilon and *All the World's a Stage* by Isaac Jackman.

---

[8] Anne Hartley Gilbert, *The Stage Reminiscences of Mrs. Gilbert* (New York, 1901), p. 23. Hereafter cited as *Stage Reminiscences.*
[9] Solomon F. Smith, *Theatrical Management in the West and South for Thirty Years* (New York, 1868), p. 41. Hereafter cited as *Theatrical Management.*

These two early theatrical announcements reveal that the amateur stage groups in Lexington were actively engaged in producing the popular pieces of the day. Here were two different organizations busy at the same time: the unnamed group, probably a town society, performed in the courthouse during the same week the Transylvania students held forth in an undisclosed place, possibly a hall at the university. Both productions offered two plays, a comedy followed by a farce, and both began early in the evening, at six o'clock. The courthouse performance advertised tickets for sale at seventy-five cents, "to be had at the office of the *Kentucky Gazette*." That these announced plays were not the first efforts of Lexington amateurs is revealed by a statement in one of the notices calling attention to "a considerable addition of scenery."

The Lexington courthouse was used again by an unnamed group on Thursday, November 21, 1799, for a production of Richard Cumberland's *The West Indian* and Arthur Murphy's *The Citizen,* announced in the *Gazette* on November 14. Following the pattern of the March performances, the amateurs presented a comedy followed by a farce; curtain time was six o'clock with the doors opening at five. Again there were statements concerning the addition of scenery, as well as a warning that there would be "no admittance behind the scenes." The advertising of new scenery and scenic effects became a stock phrase in newspaper theatrical notices. Bad as some of the scenery must have been, it seldom failed to get some kind of mention in the announcements. Theatre managers knew that audiences were as interested—or perhaps more interested—in what they saw as in what they heard. Later theatrical advertisements often described in detail every spectacular scene in the play along with bits of information about plot and character. The Lexington amateurs were copying an overworked style of newspaper stage promotion that had been the pattern for years in England and in the eastern cities of the United States.

The courthouse, Lexington's second, was built in 1788 of native limestone; it was "two stories high, and contained four rooms on each floor." The building stood on the site of the present courthouse, on Main Street at Cheapside.[10] Before the building of permanent theatres in the West after 1800, courthouses served as theatres for both amateur and professional performers in Pittsburgh, Cincinnati, St. Louis, Lexington, and many other towns. Samuel Drake, traveling with his stage troupe from New York to Kentucky in 1815, performed in a courthouse in Cherry Valley, New York. He set up a platform three feet high in front of the judge's desk and placed some extra seating in the room. His scenery consisted of six scenes: a wood, a street, a parlor, a kitchen, a palace, and a garden. He used folding wings, three on a side, and a painted backdrop to match.[11] No doubt the amateurs in Lexington used many of the same devices. They probably presented the plays in the ground floor room that served as the main courtroom. Certainly the scenery had to be minimal in these cramped quarters, and since there was no stage machinery, scenery had to be light and portable enough to shift easily by hand. This was probably accomplished by Drake's method, changing wings to match painted backdrops.

An examination of the plays presented by the Lexington amateurs in 1799 shows that late eighteenth-century English pieces, regardless of their literary merit, were the most popular. Although forgotten today, *He Would Be a Soldier*, a five-act comedy of intrigue, met with a great deal of success at its opening at Covent Garden in 1789 after it had been refused by Colman, manager of the rival theatre, Drury Lane. Frederick Pilon and Isaac Jackman, author of the companion piece, *All the World's a Stage*, were representatives of a school of English hack writers, journalists, and sometime playwrights.

The *West Indian* by Richard Cumberland is by far the best known of the plays presented in Lexington in 1799. Although it represents Cumberland's best efforts, it contains the typical,

[10] J. Winston Coleman, Jr., *The Court-Houses of Lexington (Fayette County, Kentucky)* (Lexington, 1937), p. 11.
[11] *Dramatic Life*, pp. 7-8.

contrived plot of virtue overcoming vice, resulting in the happy ending. It played to crowded London houses for thirty nights in 1771.

Arthur Murphy's *The Citizen* was a throwback to the style of the Restoration comedy of manners. The plot, borrowed from Molière, criticizes marriage through a melee of mixed situations. Obviously Murphy did not possess the literary skill of Cumberland, but he was another actor turned writer who knew the successful theatrical techniques of the day and made the most of them. The play has long been forgotten.

The Busy Body, sometimes written *The Busie Bodie*, was the first and greatest hit of Mrs. Susannah Centlivre, who rivaled Mrs. Aphra Behn as one of the first English women of letters. This play won such acclaim in the eighteenth century that the two patented theatres in London performed it in competition against each other in 1710.

So far as the earliest newspaper records show, the eight plays produced in Kentucky—one tragedy, three farces, three comedies, and one musical afterpiece—constitute western stage activity before 1800. In *The Literature of the Middle Western Frontier* Ralph Leslie Rusk mentions some military and civic entertainment by American soldiers stationed at Detroit in 1798; some of this entertainment, according to "uncertain authority," may have been dramatic.[12] But with the exception of the French-speaking theatre in New Orleans, Kentucky was the only drama-producing area of the West during this early period.

[12] Rusk, *The Literature of the Middle Western Frontier*, 2 vols. (New York, 1925), 1: 361.

* 3 *

The First Permanent Theatres

ON TUESDAY, May 19, 1801, the word *theatre* appeared
for the first time in a Lexington newspaper, *Stewart's
Kentucky Herald*. The notice stated that a performance
of *The School for Arrogance* and *The Farmer* would be presented in the theatre on Thursday evening, May 21. Although
the announcement gave the usual information concerning the
six o'clock curtain, the fifty-cent ticket price (tickets at "Mr.
Thomas D. Owing's store"), and the "No admittance behind
the Scenes" warning, there was no mention of the location of
this theatre. The 1801 notice nevertheless is the earliest reference to a theatre in the West. (Five months later, amateurs
in Cincinnati announced a performance of *The Poor Soldier* in
a theatre.)

That this Lexington theatre had been in operation for some
time is apparent from the matter-of-fact information in the
notice. Nothing is said of its being a new establishment or of
its having any kind of grand opening; the announcement is
a routine one, the kind used in notices of past performances.
The unlocated theatre may have been Saunders's exhibition hall
next to Coleman's Tavern, or it may have been an entertainment
room in one of the inns. Later, theatrical performances took
place in Henry Clay's Traveller's Hall Hotel, located on the
public square directly opposite the front of the courthouse. One
building on the corner of Water and Limestone streets, later
called the Hotel Theatre, may have been the theatre referred
to in the notice of 1801. It was used sporadically for perform-

ances until about 1810, when it was converted into a boarding house for actors.[1] No further performances occurred in the Lexington courthouse after an announcement on January 1 in the *Gazette* stating that plays would no longer be allowed in that building.[2] Not only did the city officials pass ordinances against drama performances in the courthouse, but at the same time, March 1801, Transylvania University banned all student participation in stage activity: "Resolved that no student belonging to Transylvania University, shall, under any pretense whatever, engage or assist in any theatrical performance, nor even be there unless permitted by the board of trustees, and that a copy of this resolution be annexed to the laws of the University until the next slated meeting of the Board."[3] Later the city of Lexington passed an ordinance prohibiting any moneymaking theatrical performance by individuals or groups, male or female—puppet shows, tumbling, rope- or wire-dancing, balancing, and all representations, fictitious or real. However, permission for such performances might be granted by the Board of Trustees after the payment of a sum of money to the town treasurer. Organizations sponsoring theatrical performances for various charitable causes were not subject to this law. Those who violated the decree were to be fined ten dollars for each offense.[4]

On January 1, 1802, the *Gazette* announced for January 14 a performance of *The Gamester* and *The Dead Alive*; both could be seen at the "Theatre in Lexington" for the price of fifty cents. Like the notice in 1801, this one mentioned neither the place of the theatre nor the name of the sponsoring group. With the exception of the two different curtain times (one at six and the other at seven) and the two different ticket offices, the notices were similar.

[1] Charles Staples, "The Amusements and Diversions of Early Lexington" (manuscript, Lexington Public Library, 1925), pp. 22-23.
[2] Helen Langworthy, "The Theatre in the Lower Valley of the Ohio," Ph.D. diss., State University of Iowa, 1926, p. 80.
[3] "Record of the Proceedings of the Board of Trustees of Transylvania University: 1799–1810" (manuscript, Transylvania University Library, Lexington, Ky.), March 11, 1801, p. 12.
[4] *Gazette*, 20 June 1809.

After these two performances in 1801 and 1802 no theatrical announcements appeared in the Lexington newspapers until 1807. That both the town and the university had decided to restrain the production of plays is evident; this was probably the cause of the dearth of stage activity during these years. What had happened during the earlier performances to justify these rather harsh proclamations is not known. Perhaps the charlatans had cheated some of the gullible folk, or the amateur performances may have brought down the wrath of the puritan fathers against the sinful theatre. Whatever the cause, Lexington was without drama from 1802 to 1807. Later both amateur and professional groups managed to perform within the law by giving regular benefit presentations for local worthy causes, such as bridgebuilding and the purchase of military equipment.

The four plays presented in the unlocated Lexington theatre in 1801 and 1802 are almost uncannily alike. *The School for Arrogance,* an adaptation from the French by Thomas Holcroft, is a sentimental, melodramatic piece that preaches against gambling and sin in general. Holcroft is better known for *The Road to Ruin,* another polemic on the evils of gambling. *The Farmer, or The Affrighted Child,* a comic opera by John O'Keeffe, served as the afterpiece to *The School for Arrogance.* O'Keeffe, a popular writer of comic operas, employed a production-line technique in turning out many of these sentimental musicals. His *The Dead Alive, or The Double Funeral* followed Edward Moore's *The Gamester* on the 1802 program. No fewer than three plays of the period carried the title *The Gamester.* The most popular of the three, by Moore, was first performed at Drury Lane in 1753. Moore's play is a domestic tragedy involving a gambler named Beverley (a favorite stage name of the period), who is doomed by fate and deceived by a false friend, Stukely. No theatre season of the period was complete without at least one showing of *The Gamester.* Forgotten today, it had choice roles for Garrick, Kemble, and Mrs. Siddons in the London theatres.

The only other drama notice to appear in the Lexington newspapers before 1807 was an announcement of a perfor-

mance of Goldsmith's *She Stoops to Conquer*, at Bryan's Station
on October 23, 1806. Bryan's Station, a community five miles
northeast of Lexington, sponsored the performance in connection with the examination of the town's students before its
Board of Trustees.[5] Undoubtedly many of the amateur dramatic
societies in other Kentucky communities failed to receive publicity during this period. For example, the Mason County Court
Order Book is the only record of a performance given in the
courthouse in Washington, Kentucky, in 1807: "Upon the
petition of the Theatrical Society of the Town of Washington
it is ordered that they be permitted to act in the Courthouse
provided that they enter into Bond with the Clerk of this
Court for repairing any damages they may do this Courthouse
and remove the scenery before the next meeting of the Court."[6]

On February 28, 1807, the *Gazette* listed a performance in
Lexington for Thursday, March 12, by the Thespian Society
at Traveller's Hall Inn. These amateurs presented a comedy
by George Colman, *The Poor Gentleman*, along with an unnamed farce. The proceeds from this production and from those
of an amateur group known as the Musical Society were donated
to charity. Why Traveller's Hall was being used rather than the
theatre mentioned in the notice of 1802 is not known, but the
"Theatre" and Traveller's Hall may have been one and the same.

While Lexington amateurs were reviving drama production
in 1807, Frankfort, the capital city of Kentucky, began to show
some theatrical life. On December 2, 1807, the *Western World*,
a Frankfort newspaper, printed an announcement by the "manager of the Frankfort Theatre" thanking the citizens of the
town for their patronage after the first night's performance.
He promised them that future performances would have decor-
ative scenery and good music. Unfortunately, the manager failed
to give the names of the plays for either his first showing or
his second, scheduled for December 10. On Thursday, December
17, 1807, the *Palladium*, another Frankfort paper, announced

[5] *Ibid.*, 6 October 1806.
[6] Mason County Court Order Book F (Washington, Ky.), October 1807, p.
109.

for the same evening a performance of *The Brave Irishman, or Captain O'Blunder,* a one-act farce by Thomas Sheridan. It was followed on the program by the popular musical piece *The Padlock.* The notice offered no information about the players, the organization, the theatre, or any other production details. It substituted the term "proprietor" for the word "manager."

Fragmentary as this information is, it reveals some interesting developments. Here was an attempt on the part of a manager or proprietor to organize a regular, if brief, season of productions in a place called a theatre. Since the first regular theatre in Frankfort was not built until 1811, the performance given in 1807 must have taken place in Mrs. Love's House or in Price's Friendly Inn at the Sign of the Buck. Both of these inns advertised theatrical performances, one in 1809, the other in 1811, before the opening of the Frankfort Theatre. The manager or proprietor of the theatre who advertised in 1807 was probably also the owner of the tavern where the performance took place.

Charles R. Staples, a Lexington historian, states that from 1806 to 1816 Luke Usher, a Lexington businessman, controlled the only theatre in Lexington, as well as the one in Frankfort and the one in Louisville.[7] Staples may be a little early with his date for the beginning of Usher's theatrical control in Kentucky. Since Usher did not arrive in Kentucky until 1806, he would have had difficulty controlling three theatres during that same year, especially since no regular theatres existed in any of these towns until 1808, the year he erected his theatre in Lexington.[8] He may have controlled or sponsored stage activity in Frankfort and Louisville as early as 1808, but it is doubtful. Between 1807 and 1810 Frankfort had only a few scattered performances by amateurs in taverns. The *Louisville Directory for the Year 1832,* the first city directory, states that Louisville's first stage activity occurred about 1808 and that it was organized by a group of citizens who erected a "small establishment" on the north side of Jefferson Street between Third and Fourth streets.

[7] Charles Staples, *History of Pioneer Lexington* (Lexington, Ky., 1939), p. 35.
[8] *Gazette,* 11 October 1808.

According to the *Directory* this first Louisville stage enterprise was unsuccessful; for "want of a capable management it gradually sunk into nothingness."[9] Although this Louisville theatre had amateur performances as early as 1808, it had no recorded season of plays until 1814. Had Usher controlled the drama production in Frankfort and Louisville as early as 1806 or 1808, he probably would have advertised the performances in the same manner as he did in Lexington in 1808.

According to the *Gazette* of January 5, 1808, the Thespian Society of Lexington used Traveller's Hall again on Wednesday, January 6, for a production of Thomas Morton's sentimental melodrama *Speed the Plough* and a musical farce called *The Review, or The Wag of Windsor.*

Nine months later, on October 12, 1808, the most important theatrical event in the early West occurred: the opening of Luke Usher's New Theatre in Lexington. On that day the *Gazette* announced the opening production by the Thespian Society—a comedy, Richard Cumberland's *The Sailor's Daughter*, and a farcical afterpiece, Colman's *Ways and Means, or A Trip to Dover.* Both plays had repeat performances on Saturday, October 15.

With the opening of the New Theatre western stage production moved toward a new development. Although western newspapers had used the word "theatre" in notices before 1808, they had referred to taverns or temporary, makeshift structures: amateurs performed in a Cincinnati theatre in 1801, which was described as a converted stable "between a ragged roof and a sorry floor,"[10] and Louisville's first theatre, according to one historian, was "little better than a barn" before the arrival of the Drakes in 1816.[11] Noah Miller Ludlow, who performed with the Drake Company in Lexington during the 1816 and 1817 seasons, recorded an unfavorable impression of Usher's theatre in *Dramatic Life As I Found It*, but despite his description of its faults, the building was the only permanent western theatre

[9] *Louisville Directory for the Year* 1832 (Louisville, Ky., 1832), p. 139.

[10] *Western Spy*, 10 October 1801.

[11] Henrico McMurtrie, *Sketches of Louisville and Its Environs* (Louisville, Ky., 1819), p. 126.

for a number of years. Furthermore, Luke Usher, beginning with amateurs in this building, was largely responsible for organizing the first theatrical circuit in the West.

On Tuesday, October 18, 1808, the *Gazette* described the opening of Usher's theatre:

> On Wednesday last the new Theatre lately erected by Mr. Usher in this town was opened, with the comedy of *The Sailor's Daughter*, and *Ways and Means* as an afterpiece. (By Thespian Society,) which were again repeated on Saturday evening, and to a respectable and brilliant house on both nights. The audience were gratified on their entrance of the Theatre, with a species of accommodation not heretofore known in this country—convenient and safe seats, separated as in theatres in the Atlantic cities. They were also pleased with the plan and decorations of the theatre, which do much credit to the judgment of the proprietor, Mr. Usher, and with the scenery, which competent judges pronounce to equal what is seen in the eastward, and for which we are indebted to the taste of Mr. Beck.—With respect to the performance, making due allowance for youth and inexperience, we can say it was respectable, and that the audience enjoyed much pleasure.
>
> We cannot quit this subject, without congratulating the lovers of the drama, and the friends of morality, upon the success of the first attempt which has been made to introduce a Theatre in the western country. The fastidious and cynical may regret it—but the liberal minded and enlightened portion of society must be pleased. An entertainment, innocent and instructive, which makes us moralize whilst we enjoy pleasure, which brings home to the bosoms of men the works of genius, of learning and poetry, of such men as Addison and a Johnson, of a Dryden and Shakespeare, can have no other effect than to refine and polish, and amend the morals of society. Such have been the impressions of every enlightened people, and such are ours.

Although this reporter failed to describe in detail the interior of Usher's building, an earlier account in the October 11 *Gazette* mentioned that it was completed in a "very handsome style." That it had all the structural features of late eighteenth-century theatres is certain since the *Gazette* article also announced that the pit tickets sold for 50¢, the boxes for 75¢, and the gallery for 37½¢. Servants could witness the play from the gallery, but no servant was admitted without a pass. Apparently Usher had abolished the practice of allowing servants, who held seats for others, to have free seats in the gallery. On performance nights Usher opened the doors of the theatre at five o'clock to allow the audience time to gather for the opening curtain at six-thirty. The box office opened at nine in the morning and closed at one in the afternoon.

Luke Usher had purchased the theatre property for $250 in September 1807 at a courthouse sale. The property, located on the northwest corner of High and Spring streets, had belonged to William McBean, who was forced to sell "by virtue of two executions issued from the clerk's office of the Fayette Circuit Court."[12] Usher's newly acquired property, for which he did not finish paying until November 1809, measured 66⅔ feet to the east on High Street, 222 feet north to Water (Vine) Street, and 66⅔ feet west "to Jacobus' lot." This lot, though long and narrow, may have been widened by Usher's acquisition of other High Street property in 1806 and 1807.[13] Staples says that Usher sold his umbrella business and built a brewery on the southwest corner of Vine and Spring streets, later the site of his first theatre.[14] (Since the theatre occupied the entire block, its location was at Vine and Spring as well as High and Spring.) Ludlow verifies that Usher first operated the building as a brewery,[15] but the *Gazette* of March 13, 1810, indicates that Usher did not sell his umbrella shop until March 1810.

Ludlow's description of the building, although far from complimentary, is more favorable than his accounts of theatres in Pittsburgh, Louisville, and other towns in the West and South:

> On our arrival at Lexington, many of us were surprised to find in the principal town of the State the poorest specimen of a

[12] Fayette County Court Deed Book C (Lexington, Ky.), September 1807, p. 1.
[13] Ibid.; ibid., Book B, August 1807, p. 468.
[14] Staples, *History of Lexington*, p. 35.
[15] *Dramatic Life*, p. 89.

theatre. I was informed the building had been a brewery, in which Mr. Luke Usher, the uncle of Noble L. Usher, had once conducted his business as a brewer of malt liquors. The second story of this building, a long and narrow one, had been fitted up for dramatic performances by an amateur society. It was probably seventy to eighty feet in length by about twenty-five to thirty feet in width. If I remember rightly, the seats were constructed upon the amphitheatre plan,—gradually rising from the floor, one above the other, to the back, these back seats being reached by a sloping platform at one side. They were simply covered with canvas and painted, without being stuffed or having any backs to them, and the surroundings were of the most simple and unpretending character. The stock of scenery was very limited, and not very well painted. The building stood on an abruptly rising piece of ground, and the audience entered from a street nearly on a level with the floor of the second story. Adjoining this end of the building was a room for the sale of beer and other equally refined refreshments. Underneath the stage were the dressing-rooms for the performers; into these they entered by a door that opened upon a cross-street. The dressing rooms were comfortable enough, and quite equal, in fact, I may say superior, to some in theatres of greater pretensions.[16]

From Ludlow's recollections one can conjecture about the size of the theatre itself. If the second floor measured only about 80 feet in length, the theatre was a small auditorium occupying only a fraction of the 222 feet of ground space. However, Ludlow may have been incorrect in his calculation, or he may not have included the space required by the stage and the refreshment room. Furthermore, the width must have been more than 30 feet since the lot was over 60 feet wide. Spring Street today is an "abruptly rising piece of ground" from Vine (Water) Street south to High Street. Audiences in 1808, entering nearly on a level with the second floor, must have entered on High Street, and actors found their dressing rooms underneath the stage through a lower entrance on Spring or Water Street. When Usher advertised the theatre for lease in 1819, he claimed that

[16] Ibid.

it could earn $600 or $700 a night,[17] a sum which, if not exaggerated, represents between 500 and 600 people.

Usher's opening also caught the attention of William Dunlap, a playwright and one of America's earliest stage historians. Copying verbatim from the opening announcement in the *Kentucky Gazette,* October 18, 1808, Dunlap unfortunately confused Luke Usher with his son, Noble Luke Usher:

> In October, 1808, Mr. Usher, whose name has occurred as a member of the Boston company, opened a theatre in Lexington, Kentucky, with "The Sailor's Daughter," and "Ways and Means," the characters performed by the "Thespian Society." The Theatre is mentioned as superior to former accommodations of the kind: and it is said in the western journals, "The plan and decorations do credit to the judgment of the proprietor, Mr. Usher, as does the scenery, which competent judges pronounce equal to what is seen to the eastward." The "lovers of the drama" are congratulated, and the friends of morality, upon this first attempt which has been made to introduce a theatre in the western country.[18]

Luke Usher had never been a member of the Boston Company. His son had been a member of that company beginning in 1806, but if he performed in Lexington with amateurs at his father's theatre in 1808, his name did not appear in the notices; in fact, the *Gazette* failed to mention any names except those of Beck, the scenic artist, and Luke Usher, the proprietor. Dunlap's error began a succession of confused and erroneous accounts of the Ushers and of their contributions to the early western stage by historians and stage personalities who copied Dunlap or copied someone who had copied Dunlap.

Although he did not refute Dunlap's assumption that Luke Usher was an actor, Ludlow was quick to take issue with Dunlap's statements about the Lexington Theatre: "In consequence of the favorable notice of the Lexington theatre copied from

[17] *Gazette,* 14 October 1819.
[18] William Dunlap, *The History of the American Theatre* (New York, 1832), p. 348.

Mr. Dunlap's book, my readers may be expecting me to speak in very eulogistical terms of it. I would be glad to do so, would the facts, as they appeared to me, justify it. Had Mr. Dunlap seen the Lexington theatre, instead of taking reports of partial persons, as he has done in relation to that and other theatrical matters West and South, I am sure that he would have made some very different records."[19] American theatrical histories, for the most part, devote little space to theatrical development in the early West before 1820, and often the cursory treatment given to this period comes from Ludlow's account. Dramatic activity, however, began years before Ludlow's trek west with the Drake family. We have seen that it had been stirring among Kentucky amateurs as early as 1790, but it developed further with Luke Usher's activity in Lexington in 1808 and in other areas of Kentucky in 1811, when Usher was joined by his son.

Little is known about Luke Usher before his arrival in Lexington in 1806. The *Gazette*, April 5, 1806, under the heading "Umbrella Manufactory," announced that Luke Usher from Baltimore had moved his factory to Lexington at The Sign of the Umbrella next to Traveller's Hall. Staples says that he was born in southern Ireland and as a young man moved to London, where he performed at the Covent Garden and Drury Lane theatres between 1780 and 1794; by 1799 he had emigrated to Philadelphia, where he married a widow named Ann Adams. The following year he moved to Washington, D.C., and acted at the opening of the theatre there.[20] Luke Usher may have been born in Ireland, and he may have been an actor in England; but the actor who performed in Washington, D.C., in 1800 was Noble Luke Usher, the son of Luke Usher. Because Noble Luke Usher performed under his father's name, the two were often confused.[21]

[19] *Dramatic Life*, p. 89.
[20] Staples, "Amusements," p. 22.
[21] Despite his acquaintance with Luke Usher, Ludlow refers to Noble Luke Usher as the nephew of Luke Usher; since for years Ludlow was the standard source of early western stage information, the two Ushers became known as uncle and nephew. Stronger evidence, however, reveals that Noble Luke Usher was the son of the Lexington businessman and his first wife. In 1808 John Bernard,

Luke Usher was a businessman who was active in civic affairs. He was interested in the theatre as a business venture; it is possible that he had firsthand information about theatre management since his son was an actor. In March 1819 his inn, The Sign of the Ship, burned, and during the same year he had to mortgage his theatre building to Robert Wickliffe.[22] Unable to pay his debt to Wickliffe, Usher lost his theatre property at public auction on November 8, 1825. (The notice in the *Reporter* on September 5, 1825, stated that the theatre with its dwelling house was a "very valuable establishment, and is located at one of the most advantageous places in the Western Country for a Theatrical Company; the buildings are of brick and might be adapted to various purposes.") He died at the age of seventy-two on December 23, 1829.

That Luke Usher had conceived plans for his theatre and for a Kentucky circuit as early as the spring of 1808 is certain from John Bernard's account of his correspondence with Usher. Usher had written to Bernard at least twice asking him to come to Kentucky and manage a circuit. Bernard refused because of prior commitments and because "the great distance to the back countries suggested a hundred difficulties."[23] Noble Luke Usher was then in Boston recruiting actors for his Quebec Company, but apparently Bernard said nothing to the young actor about the father's plans in Kentucky. Unable to recruit a professional company, Luke Usher began with amateurs.

Luke Usher and his unnamed amateurs sponsored four other productions in 1808 after the October 15 repeat performance of *The Sailor's Daughter* and *Ways and Means*. On Wednesday, October 19, the Thespian Society announced a performance of the celebrated five-act play *Lovers' Vows, or The Natural*

---

manager of the Boston Theatre, recruited Noble Luke Usher for his company. Bernard recalls that during the same year he received letters from Noble Luke Usher's father in Kentucky urging Bernard to manage Luke Usher's Kentucky theatres. On December 3, 1811, a scene designer named Jones who worked for Luke Usher mentioned in a complaint to the *Lexington Reporter* that Luke Usher's son had come to Lexington.

[22] Fayette County Court Deed Book S, March 1819, pp. 149-50.
[23] *Retrospections of America*, p. 336.

Son, an adaptation of Augustus von Kotzebue's drama by Elizabeth Inchbald. It was followed on the program by a dramatic entertainment entitled *As It Should Be*. Proceeds from this production went to charity or "other useful purposes." Three weeks later, on Saturday, November 5, the Thespians repeated the favorite *Speed the Plough* along with an unnamed farce. Four days later they presented another showing of *Speed the Plough*, followed by the farce *The Devil to Pay, or The Wives Metamorphos'd*, an adaptation by Charles Coffey and John Mottley of an English seventeenth-century play by Thomas Jevon. Luke Usher ended his first theatrical venture in Lexington with a performance on Wednesday, December 14, of M. G. Lewis's popular melodrama, *The Castle Spectre, or The Mystery of Conway Castle*.[24] One of the first Gothic thrillers, it was largely responsible for the introduction of melodramatic horror plays into the English playhouses. Lewis was popularly known as "Monk" Lewis from the title of his Gothic novel *The Monk*.

With the exception of *Speed the Plough*, all the amateurs' offerings were new to Lexington audiences. *Ways and Means, or A Trip to Dover*, Colman's comedy in three acts, uses the traditional formula of intrigue with lovers and comic servants; a Dover inn provides the scene for farcical mixup and mistaken identity. *Ways and Means* had become a standard piece after its debut at the Haymarket Theatre in London in 1788. The companion piece, *The Sailor's Daughter* by Richard Cumberland, was a much newer comedy; in fact, it had first been produced only four years earlier, in 1804, in London. Displaying much more moral sentiment than comedy, *The Sailor's Daughter* is a complicated bit of nonsense employing a quack doctor named Hartshorn and other characters called Captain Sentamour, Sir Matthew Moribund, and Varnish. *Lovers' Vows*, Mrs. Inchbald's popular sentimental drama, uses every melodramatic device, including seduction and robbery. A typical scene shows the reconciliation of Theodosia and Baron Wilden-

[24] *Gazette*, 18 October, 6 December 1808.

hain, her wayward lover. Frederic, their illegitimate son, has
saved his mother from illness and starvation:

> BARON: Theodosia! Know you not my voice?
> THEODOSIA: Wildenhain!
> BARON: Can you forgive me?
> THEODOSIA: I forgive you!
> FREDERIC: I hear the voice of my mother!—Ho! Mother! Father!

The Devil to Pay, an inane domestic farce, employs the devil's
spirits to resolve a contrived domestic problem.

Ridiculous as these plays appear to the modern reader, they
were appealing not only to the pioneer audiences but also to
those of London and of the eastern theatres in America. *The
Castle Spectre, Speed the Plough*, and *Lovers' Vows* were among
the most often played pieces of the period.

Except for the first reviewer's statement that the amateurs
performed well, "with due allowance for youth and inexperi-
ence," none of the newspaper notices during this first Lexington season offered any reviews or made any comments concerning the productions.

Usher's theatre was not heard from again until the spring
of 1809, when the *Gazette* announced on Tuesday, April 11, a
performance for Saturday, April 15, of a favorite farce adapted
from the French by Mrs. Inchbald—*Animal Magnetism, or
The Doctor Outwitted*. It was followed by a stock musical afterpiece, *No Song, No Supper* by Prince Hoare. Two weeks later
(Monday evening, April 24, 1809) the Lexington amateurs presented an ambitious program with Richard Cumberland's sentimental play *The Jew, or The Benevolent Hebrew*. Two afterpieces followed: Colman's one-act "occasional drama" *Sylvester
Daggerwood, or The Mad Dunstable Actor* (also known as
New Hay at the Old Market) and a pantomime *The Merry
Girl, or The Shaking Quakers*. William Dunlap's adaptation
Tell Truth and Shame the Devil headed the bill on Monday
evening, May 8, 1809, and William Macready's farce of intrigue
The Irishman in London, or The Happy African concluded the

entertainment. According to the notice in the *Gazette* on May 6, this was the "last night but one of performing."

A *Gazette* announcement on December 18, 1810, welcomed back a strolling actor named James Douglas "after an absence of eighteen months." If he had visited Lexington eighteen months earlier, he would have been performing sometime in June 1809, but no stage notices appeared in the June newspapers. He may have been assisting the amateurs beginning in April 1809, but the newspapers failed to announce any players' names until May 1810.

Despite the Lexington ordinance prohibiting drama productions, the amateurs continued regular performances throughout the 1809 season. Permission may have been granted to Usher in return for his donations to worthy causes; a theatrical notice in the *Gazette* on August 1, 1809, stated that the proceeds from the August 5 performance would go to the building of a bridge across Water and Spring streets. This production was the ever-popular *Douglas*.

During the fall of 1809 the Thespian Society performed a total of six plays on three different nights, beginning on Saturday, September 23, with Thomas Morton's spectacular play *Columbus, or The World Discovered*. Charles Shillito's musical farce *The Man of Enterprize* was the second piece. *Columbus* was repeated by "particular desire" on September 30 and October 7, but the musical afterpiece *Children in the Wood* replaced *The Man of Enterprize* as the second play. A benefit for the library of Lexington brought the Thespian Society back to Usher's theatre on October 28, 1809, for a repeat performance of *Speed the Plough* and *Children in the Wood*. Messrs. Godfrey and Plain, teachers of music at The Sign of the Green Tree, provided the orchestra for *Children in the Wood*.[25]

Children in the Wood by Thomas Morton is an example of the melodramatic, operatic genre that developed as popular entertainment in the theatres of the eighteenth and nineteenth centuries. The two-act piece comes from an old Welsh ballad

25 *Gazette*, 26 September 1809; *Reporter*, 28 October 1809.

about two children who are left in the woods to die. Morton
gave the tragic ballad a happy ending by having the children
heroically rescued. One of the songs from the original ballad
has survived. This writer recalls his mother singing it to him:

> Oh, don't you remember a long time ago,
> Two poor little babes whose names I don't know,
> Were stolen away on a bright summer's day,
> And lost in the woods I've heard people say,
> And when they were dead a robin so red
> Brought strawberry leaves and over them spread,
> And sang them a song the whole day long,
> Poor babes in the woods, poor babes are gone.

No theatre of the period presented only dramatic plays; almost
every production included a musical piece of some kind. Theatres had to have orchestras or at least actors who could play
musical instruments well enough to accompany actors who
could sing. The songs in *Children in the Wood*, according to
the notice in the October 8 *Reporter*, were sung in character.
It is interesting that the first performers' names mentioned in
these early notices were not those of the actors but those of
the musicians, Messrs. Godfrey and Plain.

These fifteen performances from April to November 1809
constitute the most active theatrical year witnessed thus far
by western audiences. It was an interesting array of serious
plays, spectacles, farces, comedies, and pantomimes. All the
pieces except *Douglas* and *Speed the Plough* were new to Lexington audiences. As the titles indicate, several of the offerings
were the usual light comedies and farces of sentiment and intrigue. Musical plays, ballad operas, musical afterpieces, and
burlettas had also become standard theatrical fare since the production of John Gay's *Beggar's Opera* in 1728.

Although the Thespian Society of Lexington did not perform again until March 1810, two productions were announced
by the Frankfort Theatrical Society in October 1809. The Frankfort *Western World* advertised for Thursday, October 5, a performance of a comedy, *The Heir at Law*, by George Colman,

and a farce, *Honest Thieves, or Lawful Depredation,* by Thomas Knight. A hornpipe dance by one of the "female characters" of the group concluded the program. The Frankfort players performed in the house of Mrs. Love, probably a tavern near the ferry and warehouse advertised by Thomas Love in the July 10, 1804, *Gazette.* The same newspaper announced for Monday, October 30, a presentation by the "Theatrical Society" of Morton's comedy *The Way to Get Married* and Walley C. Oulton's musical farce *The Sixty-Third Letter.* Again Mrs. Love's house served as the theatre for the amateurs.[26] Nothing in the newspapers gave any indication that Luke Usher or any of the Lexington players were involved in the Frankfort performances.

On March 14, 1810, the Thespian Society in Lexington resumed its productions with an old favorite, *The Busy Body,* along with *The Sixty-third Letter.* Both pieces were repeated on March 17. The theatre doors opened at five o'clock, and the performance began at six. The Thespian Society, assisted by the Musical Society, performed again on April 17, 1810, presenting *Blue Beard, or Female Curiosity* and *The Devil to Pay.*[27] *Blue Beard,* a spectacular operatic romance by Colman, used duets, quartets, and choruses to enhance the popular tale. If the Lexington amateurs really exhibited all the scenery described in the notice, the backstage crew must have outnumbered the performers. The *Blue Beard* announcement was the first Kentucky theatrical notice to describe in detail not only the scenic background for each act but incidents of plot as well. Both dramas had repeat performances on April 21.

The first recorded cast list, printed in the *Gazette* on May 1, 1810, shows that these performances used only amateur players. Messrs. Megowan, Wagnen, Bradford, Todd, Marsh, Pindell, and Wilson—prominent Lexington citizens—appeared in the Military Society's production of *Revenge* and *The Village Lawyer* on May 7. Bradford published the *Gazette,* Megowan operated a tavern, and Marsh sold umbrellas; the Todds were a

---

[26] *Western World,* 26 October 1809 (John J. Weisert's unpublished notes from Frankfort newspapers).
[27] *Gazette,* 13 March, 17 April 1810.

well-known Lexington family. According to Marsh's statement, a number of Lexington's young lawyers also performed with the Thespian Society at this time.[28] Women did not perform in these productions until the arrival of professional players later in the year; in fact, a scarcity of actresses was still in evidence in 1811, when one traveler wrote of his disappointment at seeing a man play a woman's role. In *Revenge* Pindell played Leonora and Master Boggs acted Isabella; Master Boggs and Master Cocks portrayed women in the second piece, *The Village Lawyer*. It would seem that, lacking women, the Lexington amateurs used young boys for female roles, just as the Elizabethans had done.

In addition to the list of players for *Revenge* and the description of scenery for *Blue Beard*, the Military Society announced some interesting bits of production information in its advertisement in the May 1 *Gazette*. Tickets sold for fifty cents, with no mention of box or pit prices; no money could be received at the door. (Apparently Usher or the amateurs intended to establish ticket sales on an advanced reservation basis only.) The Lexington drama patrons had to take their boxes the day of performance, meaning either that the boxes had to be paid for by the day of performance or that they could not be purchased until the day of performance. Persons of "colour" were not admitted. Those who had opposed stage performances and had helped pass laws forbidding theatricals could not have withheld permission for the performance of *Revenge* since its purpose was to raise money for the defense of Lexington.

The plot of *Revenge* by Edward Young is almost a direct copy of Shakespeare's *Othello*. Young took his characters and settings from the popular plays of Spanish intrigue. He substituted Don Alonzo for Othello, Zanga for Iago, Leonora for Desdemona, and Don Carlos for Cassio. As in most heroic tragedies, the women had little to say, a tradition that must have delighted the men playing the female parts. The afterpiece, *The Village Lawyer*, is a translation and adaptation by

28 "The Theatre in the Lower Valley of the Ohio," pp. 6-7.

William Macready of a fifteenth-century French farce, *Maistre Pierre Pathelin.*

On May 15, 1810, the *Gazette* published an interesting financial statement in connection with the production of *Revenge* and *The Village Lawyer.* It was the first detailed financial report of a theatre operation in Kentucky and probably the first in the early West:

To cash Usher rent of theatre 2 nights without the bar	$50
To do paid Marsh's ac't for performance	20
To do pd. do. for copying Revenge	10
To do pd. do's ac't for expenses of rehearsals	12.25
To do pd. do's ac't for do. at performance	7.50
To do Pd. wardrobe	7.25
To do pd. liquor	10.75
To do pd. for printing	19.75
To do pd. door keeper, servants, barbers, Ec.	12.75
To do pd. for Musick	8
To balance in Treasurer's hands	117.25
	———
CR.	275.75
By cash rec'd first night	169.00
By do second night	106.00
	$275.00

By order of the Society,
Thomas H. Pindell,
Treasurer

This financial statement reveals several interesting facts. Not only did the amateurs do well with their $275 proceeds from two performances, but Usher received the largest share in addition to the profits from the bar. More was spent on liquor than was spent for wardrobe, music, barbers, or copying. Exactly what Marsh was paid for is not known; besides acting he may have helped with the production. His name occurs in later notices with those of Usher's professional performers. He married Usher's stepdaughter and was the grandfather of Charles R. Staples, the Lexington historian who is quoted in this study.[29]

29 Ibid.

Staples says that the Military Society gave several performances to earn money for the Lexington Light Infantry's equipment.

The Lexington amateurs finished a busy season with four productions in May, June, July, and August. On May 12, 1810, the Military Society repeated *Revenge* but substituted for the second play a two-act musical afterpiece, *A House to Be Sold*, an adaptation by James Cobb of a French piece, *Maison à Vendre*. On June 6, 1810, the Military Society, having obtained Usher's theatre on better terms than before, presented Sheridan's *The Rivals*; it was followed by *A House to Be Sold*. This was the first western performance of Sheridan's classic comedy and a most ambitious choice for the amateurs, who must have been greatly challenged by difficult characterizations and some fourteen scene changes. The Thespian Society returned to the theatre on July 7 with a performance of *Abaellino, the Great Bandit, or The Venetian Outlaw*. *The Padlock* was second on the program. *Abaellino*, translated from the German and adapted for the New York stage by William Dunlap in 1802, became one of the most frequently performed of the romantic, melodramatic plays, of which there were many. Along with the announcement of *Abaellino* appeared an article which revealed that Lexingtonians were attending the theatre in large numbers. In order to accommodate more people in the front of the theatre, Usher had added boxes to the front part of the house and had converted some of the larger boxes into smaller ones, but we do not know exactly how many more people were seated. *Abaellino* had a repeat performance on July 14 along with *Children in the Wood*. The final production of the summer, on August 18, was *The Heir at Law* and O'Keeffe's farce *The Prisoner at Large, or The Humours of Killarney*.[30] The spring and summer season in 1810 gave the Lexington audiences eighteen new plays; only *The Busy Body* and *The Sixty-third Letter* had been performed before.

Luke Usher's contribution of a theatre, primitive as it may have appeared to Ludlow, was the turning point in western

[30] *Gazette*, 8 May, 5, 26 June, 3, 10 July, 18 August 1810.

stage development. Early performers in inns, courthouses, and makeshift quarters must have worked under extremely difficult conditions. Solomon Smith, one of the pioneer managers in the early West, describes a stage in Vincennes, Indiana, that was ten feet wide and eight feet deep. When the play called for bridges and mountains, Smith recalled, "we had not much room to spare; indeed, I might say that we were somewhat crowded."[31] Usher's theatre in Lexington would have seemed like Drury Lane compared to such a theatre. Joe Cowell, another pioneer actor and manager, describes one of the temporary theatres operating in Louisville as late as 1829:

> The regular theatre at Louisville, an excellent brick building, belonging to old Drake, was closed; but a cattle shed or stable had been appropriated to that purpose, and fitted up as a temporary stage. The yard, adjoining it, with the board fence heightened and covered with some old canvass, supported by scaffold poles to form the roof, and rough seats on an ascent to the back, and capable of holding about two hundred persons, constituted the audience part of the establishment, the lower benches nearest the stage being dignified by the name of *boxes*, and the upper, nearest the ceiling, the *pit*.[32]

As late as 1816, when the Drakes arrived in Louisville, they found the "regular theatre," which had been erected about 1808, to be unsatisfactory. According to Ludlow, "It was dark, dingy, and dirty. The scenery was badly painted; the *auditorium* was done in the most dismal colors, and the house badly provided with the means for lighting it."[33]

Large theatres were unnecessary in the sparsely populated early West. Cowell's description of the stable-theatre in Louisville concludes with the statement that it seated about 200. Usher's theatre in Lexington, after some years of remodeling, held about 600. Drake's new theatre in Louisville, one which

31 *Theatrical Management*, p. 41.
32 Joe Cowell, *Thirty Years Passed among the Players in England and America* (New York, 1844), p. 90.
33 *Dramatic Life*, p. 88.

had been remodeled in 1818 and rebuilt in 1828, seated about 700.[34] Nashville's new theatre, built in 1819, had a pit and two tiers of boxes which accommodated about 800. The first regular theatre in Cincinnati had the same arrangement: a pit, two tiers of boxes, and a gallery—all seating about 800.[35]

The first western theatres imitated the architecture of the larger eastern theatres, and these in turn were constructed exactly like the eighteenth-century English playhouses. Shaped like a horseshoe or an ellipse, the English auditorium contained rows of boxes placed on tiers around the sides and sometimes at the rear. Usually a gallery slanted from the rear tiers to the ceiling or replaced the second or third tier of boxes at the rear. The ground floor, the pit, contained plain benches without backs. Actors performed on an apron stage that jutted out into the pit; it was reduced in size by the end of the eighteenth century. Proscenium doors on either side of the stage opening served as entrances and exits for the actors until later in the century.[36] A front curtain was raised or drawn at the opening of the play and was used to some extent as a mask between the acts, but it was not employed for every scene change as was the custom later, in the nineteenth and early twentieth centuries. All or most of the scenery was changed before the eyes of the audience; this was part of the spectacular display. It was not until the mid-nineteenth century that curtains were employed to conceal scene changes.[37]

Scenery painted on flat wings provided a perspective view upstage to a painted backdrop. The stage was slanted, forming a ramp from the high part at the rear to the level acting apron in front. Wings slid in grooves in the floor and ceiling; they could be drawn off to show succeeding wings for a new scene. Backdrops were flown or drawn off in the same manner. Everything was painted on the scenery: doors, windows, and even

[34] *Louisville Directory for the Year 1832*, p. 139.
[35] "The Theatre in the Lower Valley of the Ohio," pp. 85-86.
[36] George Rowell, *The Victorian Theatre: A Survey* (New York, 1956), p. 15.
[37] Allardyce Nicoll, *The Development of the Theatre: A Study of Theatrical Art from the Beginning to the Present Day* (London, 1958), p. 190.

clocks (which, of course, remained at the same time throughout the play). This production technique was ideal for
spectacular pieces since scenes could be shifted quickly by
drawing off wings and changing backdrops. Theatres used
stock scenery for all plays; it usually consisted of a wood, a
palace, a throne room, a hall, and other traditional settings.
Audiences expected to see the same scenery used repeatedly.
The famous Macauley's Theatre, built in Louisville in 1873 and
supposedly modeled on the latest theatres in New York, had
a slanted stage, grooves in the stage floor and ceiling, and
twelve settings of stock scenery.[38] Offering different pieces at
almost every performance, theatre managers could not arrange
new scenery for each production, but in the established theatres
of the East they had excellent devices for changing the stock
scenery. Western theatres, mostly converted structures, had
little space for flying backdrops or for sliding scenery to the
sides of the stage. Ludlow states that in 1815 "there were very
few, if any" theatres in the West that had machinery for shift-
ing scenery; it was all done by hand.[39]

Stage lighting, the worst feature of theatre design, consisted
of wax candles and sperm oil lamps both in the auditorium and
on the stage. The Louisville Theatre in 1820 had "a grand
chandelier swung from the dome and side lights arranged along
the walls of the auditorium."[40]   Gas lighting, used in Philadelphia's Chestnut Street Theatre as early as 1816,[41] was not
employed in some of the western theatres until after 1825.[42]

Although a few great actors of the eighteenth century such
as Macklin and Garrick had experimented with a naturalistic

[38] West T. Hill, Jr., "A Study of the Macauley's Theatre in Louisville, Kentucky, 1873–1880" (Ph.D. diss., University of Iowa, 1954), p. 21. Hereafter
cited as "A Study of the Macauley's Theatre."
[39] *Dramatic Life*, p. 63.
[40] J. Stoddard Johnston, *Memorial History of Louisville from Its First Settlement to the Year 1896*, 2 vols. (Chicago, 1895), 2: 329. Hereafter cited as
History of Louisville.
[41] Arthur Hobson Quinn, *A History of the American Drama from the Beginning to the Civil War* (New York, 1946), p. 201. Hereafter cited as *A History
of the American Drama*.
[42] *History of Louisville*, 2: 329.

approach to their art, acting, for the most part, matched the declamatory, bombastic plays of the day. *Abaellino, the Great Bandit, or The Venetian Outlaw,* affords a typical example requiring heroic sweeps down the slanted stage and emotional outbursts on the part of Abaellino as he saves Rosamunda from death. (Incidentally, he saves his country as well.) This play, acted by the greatest stars of the period, was a favorite blood-and-thunder piece.

Western stage activity thus far has been a record of Kentucky performances, mainly those of Lexington. Theatrical development was almost nonexistent in other western towns before 1810, and in most instances (except in Frankfort and Louisville) before 1818.

The earliest newspaper notice of a performance in Cincinnati appeared in the *Western Spy* on September 30, 1801, but the name of the play did not appear:

CINCINNATI THEATRE
On To-morrow Evening,
Will be performed
A COMIC OPERA.

Subscribers will receive their tickets of admission by applying to Mr. Killgore.—Subscriptions not yet paid will be received by Mr. Seamons—tickets cannot be granted to subscribers who have not paid.

The managers regret, they have not had it in their power to present the subscription list so generally as they wished. Such Ladies and Gentlemen therefore, as are desirous of subscribing, are requested to send their names to Mr. Seamons.

On October 10, 1801, the *Western Spy* printed the prologue to a September 1 production of *The Poor Soldier.* Although the word "soldier" is alluded to in the prologue, the title *The Poor Soldier* does not appear. The *Bulletin* of the Ohio Historical and Philosophical Society states that this performance in Cincinnati was sponsored by a group called the Thespian Corps and was acted in a shed not far from Fort Washington. At least a part of the cast consisted of soldiers stationed at the fort.[43] Ludlow quotes a Cincinnati historian named Cist who describes the first Cincinnati theatre as a frame building on Front Street east of Ludlow Street.[44] According to Helen Langworthy, a stable owned by a man named Vattier served as the only theatre in Cincinnati before 1815.[45] This was probably the same stable mentioned by Ralph Leslie Rusk, who says that the Thespian Corps performed on an improvised stage in a stable loft a number of times in 1805.[46] Certainly the actor speaking the prologue apologizes for the theatre "all but rude" with its "ragged roof and sorry floor." The only other information concerning this first Cincinnati performance comes from a short review that appeared in the same issue of the *Western Spy* as the prologue. After naming the play and mentioning an unnamed musical interlude, the reviewer praised the scenery and the excellence of the performers, especially those (unnamed) who portrayed Fitzray, Patrick, Darby, and Bagatelle. The Program was repeated five months later on February 19, 1802.

After the auspicious and early beginning in Cincinnati the Thespians are not heard from again until 1805 when, according to Rusk, they performed a number of times from August to December in the stable loft.[47] The only other recorded performances in Cincinnati before the arrival of professional actors in 1811 occurred on Tuesday, September 30, 1806, when *Secrets Worth Knowing* and *Love-a-la-Mode* were given by the "gentlemen of Cincinnati." They returned on Thursday, December 5, 1806, with *The Mountaineers* and *The Padlock.* Tickets sold for fifty cents.[48] These few offerings constitute the known stage activity in Cincinnati from the opening announcement in 1801 to May 25, 1811.

[43] " 'The Poor Soldier'—A Revival of an Old Comic Opera to Be Staged in Cincinnati," *Bulletin of the Historical and Philosophical Society of Ohio* 9 (July 1951): 236.

[44] *Dramatic Life*, pp. 116-17.

[45] "The Theatre in the Lower Valley of the Ohio," p. 8.

[46] Ralph Leslie Rusk, *The Literature of the Middle Western Frontier*, 2 vols. (New York, 1925). 1: 355.

[47] Ibid.

[48] *Western Spy*, 23 September 1806.

One might expect that Pittsburgh, the center for pioneer travel to the West, would have sponsored theatres and acting troupes long before the communities which lay farther west. This expectation is refuted in a study by Alfred McClung Lee. Despite Pittsburgh's strategic location, it had a population of only 1,565 in 1800, and its first theatrical entertainment came from amateur groups who performed in taverns and halls. Lee gives no record of these performances. The first "regularly outfitted place for the holding of theatrical entertainment was the upper hall of Allegheny County's first courthouse." In 1805 this courthouse was changed into a theatre of a sort, and in 1808 two local dramatic societies performed *Romeo and Juliet, She Stoops to Conquer, Pizarro,* and *The Merchant of Venice* there. The first mention of a theatre in Pittsburgh, in the *Pittsburgh Gazette,* May 15, 1812, concerned the Turners, actors who had recently left Lexington and Cincinnati. The notice stated that William Turner and his company would be occupying the "New Theatre" and that subscribers were requested to pay their money to the box office keeper, Isaac Roberts.[49]

Palmer's *History of Pittsburgh* shows a picture of this theatre but gives 1817–1820 as the period of operation. However, it was probably in existence by the time of the Turner performance in 1812, for Ludlow's record of performances in this same theatre in 1815 intimates that it had been built for some time. He gave the same sweeping, unfavorable appraisal of the Pittsburgh playhouse that he gave to later ones in other areas. He also declared, as he did in many other cities, that his season with Drake in 1815 was the first regular season Pittsburgh had known.[50] Lee corroborates Ludlow's statement, concluding that Pittsburgh's first theatre was "an unpretentious structure with little public support evident." The city did not support stage activity to any great extent until 1830.[51]

Other western and southern settlements, such as St. Louis,

[49] "Trends in Commercial Entertainment," pp. 46, 122.
[50] *Dramatic Life,* p. 61.
[51] "Trends in Commercial Entertainment," p. 146.

Nashville, Detroit, and Natchez, had no recorded dramatic activity until 1815. New Orleans—not a pioneer western settlement—sponsored its first English-speaking drama on April 26, 1806, in Moore's Building on Chartres Street. A man named Rannie, who had performed magical feats the year before in Lexington, acted in *The Doctor's Courtship* and *Don Juan.* On May 7 he announced a performance of *A New Way to Pay Old Debts* and *The Unfortunate Gentleman;* he concluded with acts of ventriloquism and a spectacular demonstration of "cutting off and replacing a man's head without his feeling any pains."[52] Rannie finished his New Orleans season with a grand spectacle called *The Battle of the Nile.* No other performances are recorded for New Orleans before 1811.

That Kentucky, especially Lexington, gave to the early West the great bulk of drama production before 1810 is obvious from the existing records. The next ten years witnessed the organization of the Kentucky Circuit and the emergence of the professional acting company, significant developments which firmly established Kentucky as the principal drama-producing center in the West.

[52] Nellie Smither, *A History of the English Theatre in New Orleans* (New York, 1967), pp. 8-9.

4

Professional Players in Kentucky

O N TUESDAY, September 11, 1810, under the heading "Theatre," the *Gazette* announced that on the following Saturday the Roscian Society would present the celebrated tragedy *Pizarro*, followed by a farce, *Honest Thieves*. Messrs. Levett and Smith, sign painters and operators of the Lexington Oil Floor Cloth Factory, furnished the scenery. Rolla, the Peruvian hero in *Pizarro*, was to be played by John M. Vos of the Montreal Theatre; Vos was also to speak the prologue and the epilogue, both written by one of the citizens of Lexington. Vos, who will be mentioned later in connection with the Lexington and Louisville theatres, was a little known strolling actor before coming to Kentucky from Montreal. Unlike the typical western stroller, he was a man of good taste who later became "a pretty good actor in tragedy heroes—rough and crude, yet attended with some signs of genius. His wife played second old women. He died in 1826."[1] After the performance of *Pizarro* the critic for the *Gazette*, September 18, wrote that Vos was an actor of much promise and that he would be a fine addition to any theatrical troupe which might visit Lexington. The same Lexington writer also complimented the beauty and fashion in the theatre, overlooking the deficiencies of the inexperienced players and praising the efforts of the Roscian Society.

On September 25, 1810, the *Gazette* printed the prologue spoken by Vos at the opening of *Pizarro*. Although spoken in the character of Rolla, the Peruvian spy, it was obviously a patriotic piece designed to accompany the elegant front curtain, which represented "American Intrepidity, or the Burning of the Philadelphia in the Bay of Tripoli by Lieutenant Decatur." Other than their heroic qualities, Rolla and Decatur had nothing in common; but the prologue and the curtain gave the performers at Usher's theatre an opportunity to display their patriotism:

PROLOGUE

Here am I come, a licens'd spy
And from yon hostile camp I fly;
To make what foes we have to dread,
Whether they're home or foreign bred.
But sure this land can never hold
A wretch that's bribed by foreign gold
In tyrant's courts, they're only known,
Who dare such monstrous acts to own.
Columbia's son! glorious name!
In seeking the bright path of fame,
Let honor, justice be your guide.
Let party spirit ne'er preside;
Like Rolla, spurn a foreign foe,
Soon shall you th' oppressor low;
Then like his, we'll bless your name,
And wondering nations sound your fame,
This night we prove the direful woes,
That might from foreign bonds have rose.
Columbians! rise in awful might,
Round the wide world, now prove your right.
To freedom, commerce, justice, truth!
To honor'd age, to manly youth!
To matron's sage, to daughter's fair!
To fruitful fields, to balmy air!
O'er ocean, hold your boundless way;
Nor king, nor tyrant e're obey!
This might uphold your country's cause,
With hands, with voice proclaim applause!

[1] *Dramatic Life*, pp. 88, 270, 287.

This gala event was the first professional production in Kentucky and the early West, even though the supporting players were amateurs. The newspapers spoke of "the rich repast which our THEATRE bills promise this evening" and praised the players' efforts. Scenery and stage decoration received their share of compliments; the front curtain, depicting the "late war with Tripoli," added especially to the splendor. *Pizarro*, a popular heroic tragedy, was a good choice on such a public-spirited occasion. Vos, however, received more praise before the performance in the September 15 *Gazette*, than after: "The name of the tragedian from Montreal (Mr. Vos) which is observed in the bills, will no doubt heighten the expectations of the audience. From the manner he supports the part of *Rolla*, we may judge of the correctness of the high recommendations with which he was received—and from the justice done *Pizarro*, we may estimate the proper claim of the society, to the name of ROSCIAN."

The September 11 *Gazette* described in great detail the scenery for this production of *Pizarro*. That the scene designer was able to carry out completely the realistic settings specified by the author is doubtful. Act one shows Elvira sleeping under a canopy, along with a view of the Spanish camp. In act two the audience viewed a bank surrounded with wild woods, rocks, the temple of the sun, a magnificent altar, and a thick forest "wild and rocky" with a torrent of water falling down a precipice bridged by a fallen tree.

According to the *Gazette* announcement, proceeds from the play went to the Lexington Oil Floor Cloth Factory for its establishment "on a more intensive scale . . . for the benefit of the western states." Thus the theatre in Lexington not only supported worthy charitable causes but also helped commercial enterprises financially.

Aside from Rannie's magic exhibitions in 1806 and a vague reference to a performance by James Douglas eighteen months prior to the arrival of Vos, John Vos was the first publicized professional actor in the West. Why Canada was the source of strolling players at this time is not known, but Canadian towns are mentioned frequently as centers for theatrical recruitment. Many of the first western players, including Noble Luke Usher and Douglas as well as Vos came from Canada, where active companies both amateur and professional, had been organized in Quebec and Montreal. Luke Usher, unable to attract professional players from the eastern theatres, probably appealed to his son, who worked the Canadian Circuit from time to time, for help in recruiting actors for his Kentucky Circuit.

Pizarro, or The Death of Rolla, was an adaptation by Sheridan of Kotzebue's *The Spaniard in Peru.* This spectacular, melo-dramatic plot depicts the resistance of the Incas to the tyranny of their Spanish conqueror, Francisco Pizarro. It starred the great Kemble and his sister, the renowned Mrs. Siddons, at Drury Lane in 1799 and played with much success throughout the early part of the nineteenth century. Vos repeated it in Lexington on September 20, 22, and 26.[2] The afterpiece, *Honest Thieves, or Lawful Depredation,* is a farce by Thomas Knight, who adapted it from *The Committee* by Robert Howard. Along with the second and third performances of *Pizarro* the Roscians added James Townley's *High Life below Stairs,* one of the standard sentimental farces of the period.

Apparently the rulings against stage performances by Transyl-vania University students were no longer in effect, for on October 4, 1810, they presented at the theatre *The Castle Spectre* and a musical farce by L. Beach, *Jonathan Postfree, the Honest Yankee.* The plays were sponsored as a benefit for the charity students at the university.[3]

The first Shakespearean production performed in Kentucky took place in Lexington as a benefit performance for Vos on October 11, 1810. *Macbeth, Tyrant of Scotland* gave him his second starring role in Lexington; he was supported by amateur performers from the community. Oddly enough, the cast list failed to mention the name of the actor who played Lady Macbeth. The brief review in the *Gazette* on October 16,

[2] *Gazette,* 18, 25 September 1810; *Reporter,* 22 September 1810.
[3] *Gazette,* 2 October 1810.

however, mentioned that the female part had been transferred to one "whose talents are better adapted to characters of that description." The player who first attempted the role was referred to as "he," an indication that actresses were still scarce. *Macbeth* drew "numerous audiences" to witness the tragic powers of Vos, but the "applause was not so general as might have been expected." He had impressed the audiences more favorably as Rolla. Something occurred during the afterpiece, the farce *Raising the Wind*, to invoke the displeasure of the *Gazette* critic, who stated that "the scandalous depiction in the farce had been remedied for Wednesday." Miss Durable, one of the performers in the farce, was to be more "honorably represented, and a more brilliant entertainment" was hoped for in the next presentation.

The second (and sometimes third) titles of these plays are interesting. Most popular plays had second titles, a convention originally meant to clarify or expand the main title. Often second titles were totally improvised, as with *Macbeth, Tyrant of Scotland* and *King Lear and His Three Daughters*. Some plays acquired such differing second and third titles that they were difficult to recognize, especially when they were advertised only by one of the many second titles. *Abaellino*, for example, was advertised by its second title, *The Venetian Outlaw*, but was also known as *The Great Bandit*, the second part of the first title.

The production of *Macbeth* ended the brief professional debut of John Vos in Lexington. He probably did not like acting with amateurs, for he left the city and did not return until the summer of 1811.

Another stroller, James Douglas (sometimes spelled Douglass), followed closely on the heels of Vos. Douglas received an enthusiastic welcome in the *Gazette*, December 18, 1810:

> It is with sincere pleasure we are at length enabled to congratulate the lovers of the Drama, and the fashionables of the town, upon the arrival of *Mr. Douglas*, with a company of *Theatrical performers* from *Montreal* and *Quebec*. After an absence of eighteen months, Mr. D. has succeeded in accom-

plishing the objects of his journey, and has engaged a company sufficiently large to form an establishment in the western country. The citizens of Lexington and Frankfort will be gratified during the present winter with their performances, which in addition to the usual amusements of assemblies &c. will contribute much to dispel the gloom of the season. The Tragedy of *Jane Shore* is proposed for the first performance in Lexington, which is expected to take place in the present week. From this very favourable manner in which they have been spoken of, they will no doubt meet with ample remuneration.

James Douglas was the son of the well-known David Douglas, the first theatre builder in the United States. Though not an outstanding actor, David Douglas was an excellent manager, and with the Hallam family he organized the first American theatrical circuit, serving most of the eastern cities. He built many theatres during his career, but he is best known for building in 1766 the first permanent theatre in America, the Southwark Theatre, in Philadelphia on South Street. There in 1767 he produced the first play written by an American and performed by professionals on an American stage, *The Prince of Parthia* by Thomas Godfrey.[4] Apparently James Douglas did not inherit his father's talent, for at about the age of fifty, when he appeared on the Lexington stage as Usher's leading actor and manager, he was a little known strolling player.

Traveling with Douglas from Canada was a small troupe of players who formed the first professional company in the early West. Sophia Turner, the leading lady, had acted in her native England at Bath and Bristol before making her debut in New York and Philadelphia. George C. D. Odell said that Mrs. Turner began her American stage career as Angela in *The Castle Spectre* at the opening of the Park Theatre in New York in September 1807. He referred to her New York debut as "a brief, inconspicuous career on these classic boards."[5] Francis C. Wemyss said that Mrs. Turner was an excellent

[4] *A History of the American Drama*, p. 16.
[5] George C. D. Odell, *Annals of the New York Stage*, vol. 2 (New York, 1927), p. 293.

actress and was for years a member of the Philadelphia stage.[6] Her husband, William A. Turner, also English, was an excellent manager who developed several of the early western stage ventures; in fact, the Turners were the first professional players to appear in Cincinnati and St. Louis. The Turners had two children, a boy and a girl, both of whom later became performers with their parents.

Little is known about the others who made the trip to Lexington with Douglas. John Cipriani was a pantomimist and a clown who had been, according to his notices, ballet master at the famous Sadler's Wells Theatre in London. John Bernard of the Boston Theatre spoke of recruiting a clown named Cipriani from the Sadler's Wells Theatre in 1806.[7] Cipriani opened a dancing school in Lexington on February 5, 1811, and divided his time between teaching and acting at Usher's theatre. He is not heard of after 1814. Kennedy and Williams, whose first names did not appear in the papers, played leading and supporting young men. Richard Jones, scenic artist for the company, also served as utility actor; his wife and Mrs. Cipriani performed supporting roles. The Ciprianis had a daughter who danced in the spectacular productions and between the plays. Later information reveals more about these performers, especially the Turners, who became important players on the western stage.

Douglas was scheduled to perform Rowe's tragedy *Jane Shore* during the week of December 18, 1810, but the *Gazette* made no mention of the specific dates. On December 22 the Lexington *Reporter* announced that Douglas would perform Mrs. Inchbald's adaptation *The Child of Nature* "for a few nights only" beginning that evening. It was to be followed on the same program by the two-act comic opera *Sprigs of Laurel, or The Rival Soldiers* by John O'Keeffe. The theatrical announcements of December 22, 1810, listed the casts of both plays, the musical entertainment between the play and the farce, the

---

[6] Francis C. Wemyss, *Chronology of the American Stage from 1752 to 1852* (New York, 1852), p. 135. Hereafter cited as *Chronology of the American Stage*.
[7] *Retrospections of America*, p. 276.

price of admission, curtain time, and even the original source for Mrs. Inchbald's adaptation.

On December 22, 1810, the *Palladium* advertised that Douglas would open an engagement in Frankfort: "We are happy to have it in our power to inform the citizens of Frankfort and its vicinity, that Mr. Douglass has at length succeeded in bringing to this place a company of Comedians. Report speaks of them very highly, and we anticipate receiving, through their means, a pleasing acquisition to our public amusements; and we doubt not that the liberal inhabitants of this place will amply reward their exertions. Due notice will be given of their first performance."

The company's last performance in Lexington before it moved to Frankfort was on Wednesday night, December 26, 1810. It was a comedy, another adaptation of a play by Kotzebue, *Reconciliation, or The Birthday*; this was followed by *The Weathercock, or Love Alone Can Stop Him* by John T. Allingham. Between the play and the farce Cipriani danced a fancy dance, Mrs. Turner recited a piece called "Jealousy," and Williams sang a comic song. It was a lengthy evening's entertainment. The Lexington reviewer, writing in the January 1, 1811 *Gazette*, reminded some of the actors of Hamlet's advice to the players, but for others he had nothing but praise. Jones was criticized for playing too much to the audience in the character of Jack Junk in *Reconciliation*, but he was considered excellent in his portrayal of Tristram Fickle in *The Weathercock*. Kennedy played with ease and judgment; Douglas was greatly improved, a remark inferring that his earlier efforts had not been impressive. The highest compliments went to Mrs. Turner and Mrs. Cipriani: "Mrs. Turner possesses considerable talents and powers, with grace, ease and elegance combined, and a person beautiful and fascinating; an audience of taste can but be interested in whatever part she may undertake. Mrs. Cipriani plays handsomely in a particular line of characters—the buffoonery and babboon capers of some of the others have been ill timed, but will do well in their proper place."

Since in 1811 Frankfort had a population of only about 1,000,[8] it was impossible for Luke Usher to consider a theatrical season there except during the winter at the time of the State Legislature meeting, usually in December and January. During this early period Frankfort had little aside from the legislature to recommend it as a theatrical town. Despite the commanding view that the countryside offered, Frankfort was described by Elias Pym Fordham in 1818 as "hidden in a mudhole."[9] A traveler named Cuming visited Frankfort in 1807, the year of the first drama announcement, and found a town of ninety houses, a statehouse, and four inns. The first permanent bridge across the Kentucky River was then under construction.[10] Frankfort had a political and literary newspaper first published in 1798, but the first regular weekly newspaper, the *Western World*, was not started until 1806. Eight months after the Douglas theatrical engagement in Frankfort, during the fall of 1811, another traveler, John Melish, visited the town and described it in more flattering language than Fordham's "mudhole" terminology:

> It is neatly laid out, the streets crossing one another at right angles, and they are mostly all paved. It consists of about 150 houses, the most of them handsomely built with brick. The public buildings are the state-house and a penitentiary aforesaid, and a bank. A theatre and a church are building. A great many of the young men are addicted to gaming, a vice that generally leads to others of a more serious nature. . . . With a view of correcting this vice a number of citizens attempted to establish a public library, but it is not succeeding, they have subscribed to build a theatre, in order to form an amusement for the ladies, presuming, I think very correctly, that a number

[8] According to Lewis Frank Johnson, the population of Franklin County in 1800 was 5,078; of that number 628 lived in the town of Frankfort. *The History of Franklin County, Kentucky* (Frankfort, Ky., 1912), p. 40. Ralph Leslie Rusk writes that Frankfort, which still had fewer than 2,000 inhabitants in 1890, had been made the seat of government in 1792. *The Literature of the Middle Western Frontier*, 2 vols. (New York, 1925), 1: 28-29.

[9] Elias Pym Fordham, *Personal Narratives of Travel in Virginia, Maryland, Pennsylvania, Ohio, Indiana, Kentucky;* . . . (Cleveland, Ohio, 1906), pp. 160-61.

[10] *Sketches of a Tour to the Western Country*, pp. 191-93.

of the most virtuous of the gentlemen will be forced in the ladies company.[11]

Despite difficulties of travel, Douglas and his troupe opened the first recorded season in Frankfort on January 12, 1811. On that day the *Palladium* announced that Douglas's production of *Lovers' Vows* and *The Weathercock* were to take place at the theatre in Price's Friendly Inn at the Sign of the Buck, located at Ann and Montgomery streets. Price probably had an entertainment hall or even a temporary theatre which Douglas utilized until the Frankfort citizens completed the permanent theatre in the fall of 1811. The Frankfort audience paid one dollar for tickets, children half price; Usher charged twenty-five cents more in Frankfort than in Lexington, a practice which later drew criticism from the Frankfort citizens. Douglas opened his doors at five-thirty, thirty minutes before the opening curtain.

The second and last performance of the Frankfort engagement occurred on January 21, 1811, with *The Gamester* and *The Waterman, or The First of August*. Whether or not the evils of gambling shown in *The Gamester* had any effect on the "gaming" habits of the Frankfort gentlemen is not known, but in his January 19 review the *Palladium* reporter, after praising Moore's play, reminded his readers that "the fate of Beverley is the most striking lesson to youth, we have ever read or seen to put them on their guard against that prevailing vice of the present day, *Gaming*." The afterpiece, *The Waterman*, is a farcical ballad opera in two acts by Charles Dibdin.

Usher's theatre, "having undergone considerable alterations, and having been newly painted by Mr. Jones," started the new year on Wednesday, January 26, 1811, with two old standbys, *Lovers' Vows* and *Love-a-la-Mode*. Usher or Douglas announced performances for Wednesday and Saturday, a schedule which the company did not follow throughout the season. Not only

[11] John Melish, *Travels in the United States of America in the Years 1806, 1807, and 1809, 1810, and 1811*, 2 vols. (Philadelphia, 1812), 2: 181-82.

did this small company have difficulty in managing two different productions of four plays in each week, but Lexington apparently could not support semiweekly performances for an extended period; after March 20 the Lexington newspapers advertised performances only for Saturdays. (Ludlow, speaking in 1816, said that none of the western theatres had performances more often than four nights a week.[12])

All was ready for the new opening, which must have been quite an occasion, not only for the citizens of Lexington, who were proud of their redecorated theatre, but for Luke Usher, whose dream of establishing a permanent professional theatre in Kentucky had come true.

Douglas began an ambitious program that kept his actors busy. Some of the so-called tragedies were long, talky pieces with many scene changes and elaborate costumes. The comedies and farces often called for singing and musical arrangements. In addition there were the usual recitations, pantomimes, dances, and a variety of between-the-acts entertainment. With the help of a small but versatile company, Douglas produced forty-three dramatic and musical pieces in twenty-one evenings of production from January 26 through August 3, 1811. Twenty-six of the plays were new to Kentucky audiences. This lengthy engagement with its variety would have been impossible had Douglas used inexperienced players or had he not been able to utilize contemporary stage practices.

American production methods came directly from British techniques of the eighteenth century. Like the stock scenery that saw repeated service, the plays, for the most part, had been stock acting vehicles in all the American theatres for years. Any actor such as Douglas or Turner who had spent years in a regular operating company, even as an extra, soon learned the system that had been standard procedure since the beginning of the century. Bad as most of these stock pieces were, they appeared on the boards time and again until most actors knew every line. Since the actors played the parts in almost the same manner at each performance, they needed little

---

[12] *Dramatic Life*, p. 82.

rehearsal; in fact, the system developed as a means to minimize the need for numerous or lengthy rehearsals. Certainly the plays were badly produced, with much prompting and ringing down of curtains on impossible scenes, but the stock system was the only answer for a company performing forty-three plays in one season, with no long runs. As late as 1875, Mary Anderson made her debut as Juliet at Louisville's Macauley's Theatre after one hasty rehearsal.[13]

The acting troupes of the day, later to be called "stock companies," utilized a method of acting known as "lines of business," meaning that an actor played the same type of stock character in almost every play. Actors were typed as heavies, juveniles, leading men and women, second men and women, utilities, and walking ladies and gentlemen. Crude as the system was, it facilitated production during seasons requiring a different play every night. If an actor could develop a strong line of business, he needed only to learn the various parts and his position was practically assured, for he played all the parts alike once he learned a "line." Lines of business changed only when actors grew too old to play juveniles or developed other physical changes which forced them to change stage character. If a great actor played Hamlet in a certain way, his style was copied for years by younger actors. Only a few actors such as Garrick and Macklin dared to be different; for the most part, acting in the eighteenth and early nineteenth centuries was an imitative, stereotyped business. As late as 1879, Clara Morris, a well-known American actress, found these lines of business as inflexible as they had been years before. In her book, *Life on the Stage*, Miss Morris describes the system: " 'Oh, I can't play that; it's not in my line!' 'Oh yes, I sing, but the singing don't belong to my line!' 'I know, he *looks* the part and I don't, but it belongs to my line!' And so, nearly every week, some performance used to be marred by the slavish clinging to these defined 'lines of business.' "[14]

On Saturday, February 9, 1811, Douglas presented a benefit

---

[13] "A Study of the Macauley's Theatre," p. 176.
[14] Clara Morris, *Life on the Stage* (New York, 1902), p. 40.

for Mrs. Turner, who played the role of Isabella in Thomas Southerne's popular tragedy of the same name. The play's second title, *The Fatal Marriage*, added a degree of suspense to the first. According to the notice in the *Reporter* of February 9, 1811, *Isabella* had been performed "upwards of one hundred nights successfully, with unbounded applause" at Drury Lane. The same newspaper printed the following sentimental line from the play: "Two husbands and not one; married to both, and yet a wife to neither." In addition to acting in the tragedy Mrs. Turner played the role of Little Pickle in the farce *The Spoiled Child* by Isaac Bickerstaffe and gave a recitation between the plays entitled "Belles Have at Ye All." Williams joined in with a comic song, "Thimble's Scolding Wife Lay Dead." Again the critic in the *Gazette*, February 19, 1811, praised Mrs. Turner for her ability to interpret different roles, for her stage knowledge and dramatic talents, which were "more extensive than usual in the interesting and laborious character of Isabella," and for her portrayal of Little Pickle, "past all praise." Jones gave a satisfying performance, and Kennedy's respectable acting was thought of as never "o'er stepping the modesty of nature."

Another adaptation from the French by Mrs. Inchbald, *The Midnight Hour, or The War of Wits*, was first performed on Wednesday, February 13, along with a farcical afterpiece, *Fortune's Frolic, or The True Uses of Riches* by John Allingham. According to the February 12 *Gazette* Jones painted a special view of the general's moonlit garden with a pavilion on each side for *The Midnight Hour*. Between the play and the farce Mrs. Turner repeated the recitation "Jealousy," and Williams sang a comic song, "Old Woman of Eighty."

Douglas presented Shakespeare's *Romeo and Juliet* on Saturday, February 23. As excellent an actress as Mrs. Turner was, she was probably too old to play Juliet to Kennedy's Romeo; however, it was the custom throughout the nineteenth century for older actresses to portray Juliet, especially if they had played the part in years past. Turner acted the supporting role of Paris, Jones performed Mercutio, and Douglas played Friar

Lawrence. Jones also designed the scenery—moonlit gardens, porticos, churchyards, and monuments. Though Shakespeare was popular, often in altered form, during the nineteenth century, his plays were not performed as much in the early West as were the eighteenth-century sentimental dramas. *Romeo and Juliet*, along with the two *Macbeth* productions by Vos, were the only Shakespearean pieces done in Kentucky by 1811.

Cipriani concluded the evening of Shakespeare with a pantomime, *Harlequin's Vagaries, or Love Triumphant,* an original, spectacular feat displaying tricks of magic that changed a milliner's box to a grate, a parasol to a gridiron, and a closet to a clock. Williams, playing Harlequin, leaped six feet in the air through the clock (that had been changed from a closet). Marsh played Pantaloon; Turner, the lover; Cipriani, the clown; Mrs. Turner, Columbine; Mrs. Cipriani, the Genius of the Wood; and Miss Cipriani, Cupid.[15] Pantomimes had been an important phase of English stage production since the time of the great Harlequin John Rich, who became the first manager and director of pantomimes at Covent Garden in 1731. Through the influence of the commedia dell' arte performers in Europe, Harlequin became the best known of the many stock characters.

On February 27 the *Reporter* announced a repeat performance of *The Midnight Hour* for that evening. Comic songs with the unusual titles "Giles Scroggins Ghost," "The Yawners," and "The Lady of France" were to be sung by Kennedy and Jones, and the program would conclude with the favorite farce *The Village Lawyer.*

Performing twice each week during March 1811, Douglas was busier than he had been at any time since his arrival in Kentucky. He gave a benefit for Williams on Saturday, March 2, with John Tobin's musical play *The Curfew, or Danish Banditti.* To this was added a two-act musical farce, *The Prize, or 2,5,3,8,* by Prince Hoare. On March 6 a benefit for Marsh featured *Secrets Worth Knowing* by Thomas Morton and *Cath-*

---

[15] *Gazette,* 19 February 1811.

erine and Petruchio, Garrick's popular alteration of Shakespeare's *The Taming of the Shrew.* Mrs. Cipriani's benefit on March 9 offered Thomas Holcroft's *A Tale of Mystery, or The Rocks of Appennez* and *The Farm House, or Female Duellist.* With the success of *Romeo and Juliet* and *Catherine and Petruchio,* Douglas was ready on March 13 for another attempt at Shakespeare—*Othello,* as adapted by the actor John Philip Kemble. Colman's *Love Laughs at Locksmiths* was the second offering. On Saturday, March 16, Douglas and Kennedy took a double benefit with Friedrich Schiller's romantic classic *The Robbers,* and Mrs. Turner repeated her portrayal of Little Pickle in the afterpiece, *The Spoiled Child.* Cipriani took his benefit on Wednesday, March 20, with *Barbarossa, Tyrant of Algiers.* He presented the last pantomime of the season, *Love and Magic, or Harlequin's Conqueror,* as an afterpiece to *Barbarossa,* a melodramatic spectacle by Dr. John Browne. *Othello* had a second showing on Saturday, March 23, along with a repeat of *Love Laughs at Locksmiths,* announced in the *Reporter* the day of the performance. Although the season was supposed to have ended in the spring, the company agreed to perform six more times; but before the summer season was over, they had given more than six extra performances.

The Lexington newspapers, notably the March 16 and March 23 *Reporter,* gave Douglas full coverage in most of the theatrical notices during this early spring season. Kennedy played the leading role in *Othello* and the part of Francis De Moor in *The Robbers.* Jones designed new scenery for *The Robbers* which displayed a tower and a cave. Doubling as actor and scene designer for *A Tale of Mystery,* Jones constructed an entirely new setting, a view of the rocks of Appennez with a bridge and a cascade of water, and acted the leading role of Barbarossa. He was supported by Mrs. Turner, who performed the heroine, Irene; Kennedy, who played Selim; and Mrs. Cipriani, who portrayed Zaphira. In addition to the two plays each evening, the audience enjoyed the usual offerings of songs and dances. After the performance of *The Curfew* Williams sang a comic song, "The Post Captain," and Kennedy sang "The Jew Broker."

Cipriani executed a hornpipe dance to conclude the program. After the showing of *Othello*, Kennedy and Jones sang more comic songs, the titles of which do not appear exactly appropriate to the occasion: Kennedy sang "Murder in Irish" and Jones presented "The Learned Pig."

The plays of the spring season represented a unique variety, ranging from dramatic classics such as *Othello* and *The Robbers* to the melodramatic spectacle of *Barbarossa. Catherine and Petruchio* was one of the most popular plays of the period; in fact, it was the only version of *The Taming of the Shrew* performed in the early western theatre. According to the February 9 *Reporter*, Holcroft's sentimental melodrama A *Tale of Mystery* had been performed in London "upwards of 60 nights, successfully, with most distinguished approbation." The play used one of the stock stories, a woman separated from her child. By the end of the play the son, now grown into a distinguished man of rank, is reunited with his mother. In Dr. John Browne's *Barbarossa* Queen Zaphira mourns the death of her husband, who has been killed by Barbarossa. In typical emotional language she refuses Barbarossa's offer of marriage: "Never! O, never—Sooner wou'd I roam in unknown exile thro torrid climes of Afric, sooner dwell with Wolves and Tygers, Than mount with thee my murder'd Selim's Throne." The renowned child actor of the nineteenth century, Master Betty, made his first appearance on the London stage in the role of Barbarossa in 1803. Though laughed at on his first entrance, he was applauded before the play was over. He became the rage of London, acting in many of the classic pieces of the period, and rivaled several prominent actors, including the great Kean.

Certainly the outstanding talent in Lexington's first professional season was Mrs. Sophia Turner, who drew exceptionally favorable notices for all her roles. She was undoubtedly the first actress of real merit to visit the West. Unknown in the theatres of the East except as a supporting player, Mrs. Turner was applauded in Lexington, Cincinnati, St. Louis, and other western cities. Seldom did a performer of wide reputation leave the comfortable life of the eastern theatres to rough it in the West.

Before 1816 Francis Blisset and Mrs. Barrett were the only well-known players to have appeared on the western stages; the others were strolling players who would have been supernumeraries in an eastern theatre. However, some actors, such as Edwin Forrest, who served their apprenticeship in western theatres later achieved greatness.

After the last production of *Othello* on March 23 the Douglas company appears to have been split by dissension. For some unknown reason—probably a financial argument with Luke Usher—the Turners and the Ciprianis decided by "mutual consent" to leave the company: "In consequence of our connextion with the company being dissolved, by mutual consent, there will be no performance in which we whose names here subscribe will be concerned in: William Turner, Sophia Turner, John Cipriani, Mary Cipriani." That the Turners did not leave the company until late in the spring of 1811 is certain, since Turner took a benefit on April 13 and Mrs. Turner performed leading roles on April 20 and May 4.[16] They moved to Cincinnati in May for a few performances, returned to Lexington in 1813 and again in 1815, and performed in St. Louis, Pittsburgh, and New Orleans from 1816 to 1819. Their theatrical wanderings after the Lexington season of 1811 will later be discussed in detail. After 1811 the Ciprianis opened several dancing schools in Lexington and played in Usher's theatre from time to time, but by 1815 they had left the West.

Despite internal strife, Douglas's company acted throughout the spring and sporadically in the summer of 1811. Benefit performances occurred in the middle of June for Jones, Douglas and Kennedy. Proceeds from the April 30 performance went for the building of the old Spring Street Bridge, which had not yet been completed. Vos, who appeared from time to time on the Kentucky stage, returned to Lexington on June 4 to assist Douglas with his depleted company. Apparently undaunted by the departure of the Turners and the Ciprianis, Douglas and Vos continued successfully in the heat of June and July and even managed to present one evening of plays in August. Not

[16] Ibid., 26 March, 4 May 1811.

only did Douglas carry on a full theatrical season during this period, but he managed to produce eleven new pieces out of the sixteen offered: Henry Fielding's *The Mock Doctor, or The Dumb Lady Cured*; Andrew Cherry's *The Soldier's Daughter*; Monk Lewis's *Adelmorn, the Outlaw*; Charles Kemble's *A Budget of Blunders*; Thomas Dibdin's *The Jew and the Doctor, or Virtue Protected*; Shakespeare's *King Henry IV, or The Humours of Sir John Falstaff*; James Kenny's *Matrimony, or Happy Imprisonment*; William Whitehead's *The Roman Father, or The Deliverer of His Country*; Theodore Hook's *Tekeli, or The Siege of Montgatz*; Charles Kemble's *Point of Honor*; and an interlude adapted from Lope de Vega, *The Father Outwitted*. Douglas repeated the old favorites *Abaellino, All the World's a Stage, The Gamester, Love-a-la-mode*, and *The Weathercock*.[17]

The Lexington newspapers continued to provide much production information. Douglas played the leading role of Andy MacSarcasm in *Love-a-la-Mode*, and Vos starred as Hotspur in *Henry IV*. Jones not only performed the leading role in *Abaellino* but also acquired special colors from Philadelphia to design spectacular scenery for the play. For act one he designed "a rude gloomy room, the retreat of the banditti," and a garden of the doge's palace in Venice, complete with rose bower. For act two he built a chamber in the doge's palace, supported with pilasters of pink marble. Mrs. Turner assumed all the leading female roles: Rosamunda in *Abaellino*, Widow Cheerly in *The Soldier's Daughter*, Imogen in *Adelmorn*, Mrs. Beverley in *The Gamester*, and Horatia in *The Roman Father*. Although Turner was more of a manager than an actor—a circumstance that may have contributed to the rift in the company—he performed regularly in supporting roles at this time. Apparently Douglas had difficulty acquiring a leading lady to replace Mrs. Turner, for he had to use an amateur in *Henry IV*, for the role of Lady Percy: "a lady, her first appearance on any stage."[18]

A glance at the new plays produced by Douglas in the spring

[17] *Gazette* and *Reporter*, 2 April to 3 August 1811.
[18] *Gazette*, 4 June 1811.

of 1811 shows that Shakespeare's *King Henry IV* and Fielding's *The Mock Doctor* are the only significant ones. However, the others, although forgotten today, were popular in all the theatres of the period. Fielding's *The Mock Doctor* was a successful musical farce taken from Molière's *Le Médecin malgré lui*. In *The Mock Doctor* a silly fake doctor attempts to cure a woman of dumbness; despite his ignorance, she recovers and talks so much that her father wishes the doctor had not been successful. Fielding is usually thought of as a successful novelist, but early in his career he was a playwright and lessee of the Haymarket Theatre. His satires brought down Walpole's wrath on the London theatres, resulting in the Licensing Act of 1737, which gave monopolies to Drury Lane and Covent Garden and placed all plays under the censorship of the Lord Chamberlain.

The Soldier's Daughter, a so-called comedy by Andrew Cherry, is nothing more than a piece of maudlin sentimentality, as can be seen in the following lines of one of the characters, Mrs. Malford: "A husband sinking beneath a load of worldly care, and a poor prattling innocent unconscious of her state, are now my sole possessions. A brother banished by his own imprudence, and my husband's father removed to climes far, far beyond inquiry, and ignorant of his son's desponding state—or, knowing it, perhaps by evil tongues, or monstrous suggestion hardened to his sufferings."

The newspapers referred to Monk Lewis's *Adelmorn* as a drama in three acts with songs added. In this heroic tale Adelmorn, suspected of killing his uncle, has turned outlaw after making an escape from prison. He is finally redeemed by his uncle, who returns as a ghost to reveal the true murderer in Hamletlike fashion. For this melodrama, made popular by Charles Kemble at Drury Lane in 1801, the scene designer constructed a gloomy prison in a castle. Adelmorn dreams that the walls separate in the center to display a desert heath with a tomblike monument on which is inscribed in crimson letters "Blood will have Blood."

A *Budget of Blunders*, originally called *Madness Rules the*

Hour, was adapted by Charles Kemble, another actor who also wrote plays. It was a popular farce employing a mixup of girls in love, a character named Smugface, and a scene in a lunatic asylum. The original Joe Jefferson, grandfather of the renowned American portrayer of Rip Van Winkle, had starred in this piece at the Park Theatre in New York a few months before the Lexington production; he had performed with a fine actor named Francis Blisset. The same Blisset appeared in the Kentucky Circuit in 1814, where he performed with Thomas Jefferson, the son of his former acting colleague.

The Roman Father by William Whitehead is a heroic tragedy influenced by the neoclassic style of the French dramatist Corneille. In this melodramatic story of love and honor in ancient Rome, a Roman father declaims endlessly in favor of his sons' dying for their country; his wish is fulfilled when two of them fight each other in mortal combat. The play is nothing more than a series of long speeches on bended knee by the father, the sons, and one son's wife. The characters have the interesting names of Horatia, Horatius, and Valeria.

The Jew and the Doctor, another of Thomas Dibdin's contrived little farces, uses the wornout story of a father who wants his son to marry one girl while the son wants another—in this play, a foundling of an old Jew. The happy ending is as contrived as the rest of the plot.

James Kenny's "petite opera" in two acts, *Matrimony,* is an adaptation from a French piece called *Adolphe et Clare.* It is a musical afterpiece with a ridiculous plot about a man and his wife who work out their marital problems by sentencing themselves to prison in a castle. The finale finds them singing:

> May love and reason ever reign
> In each fond heart with gentle sway;
> And may you never need again
> The friendly lessons of to-day.

That the great majority of these plays are extremely trite, silly, melodramatic, and immature is obvious from the snatches of the plots given here. Why then were they performed over and over again? Why were they chosen in preference to the Elizabethan tragedies or the clever Restoration comedies? The answer can be found in the differences between the seventeenth-century audience and audiences of the eighteenth and nineteenth centuries. The first was a select, upper-class group that demanded sophisticated drama. The latter were primarily middle-class audiences seeking contrived happy endings, slapstick farces, sentimental comedies, musical afterpieces, and domestic tragedies.

An especially good example of the kind of play which appealed to eighteenth- and nineteenth-century audiences is *Tekeli, or The Siege of Montgatz,* a melodrama by Theodore Hook. Lexington audiences could witness in this piece Tekeli, the Hungarian hero, and Wolf, his true friend, who saves Tekeli's wife from perilous dangers as storms hover over the romantic castle of Montgatz. The play combined all the heroic elements, including music, and was successfully produced at both patented theatres in London.

Although Douglas's 1811 season in Lexington and Frankfort was the longest and most successful that the West had known, there were those who continued in their outspoken belief that the drama was nothing more than an instrument of vice. The *Gazette* of April 23, 1811, printed a diatribe by a Transylvania student named William L. Brown, who stated that the theatre had occupied almost exclusively the attention of Lexington youth and that this trend had produced alarming consequences. According to Brown, the theatre was an ally of vice, or artful sophistry; it weakened the ties of virtue, and habitual attendance produced habitual enervation. He warned the people of Lexington to abstain from attending the theatre and compared it to a robber who would steal their richest possessions. Apparently, few paid much attention to him, for the theatrical enterprise in Lexington developed further from 1811 to 1815 than in all the previous years put together.

During the summer of 1811 the Turners and the Ciprianis operated in Cincinnati at a theatre advertised "near the Colum-

December 17, 1808.

A LIVING ELEPHANT

TO be seen at the house of Wm. Satterwhite from Tuesday the 20th to Saturday the 31st instant. Those that wish to gratify their curiosity by seeing the wonderful works of nature, will do well to call previous to that time. Perhaps the present generation may never have the opportunity of seeing an Elephant again, as this is the only one in the United Sates, and perhaps the last visit to this place.

The Elephant is eight years old and is upwards of seven feet high.

☞ Admittance 25 Cents. To be seen from 9 o'clock in the morning till sunset.

44   Dec. 12.

Satterwhite's Inn notice,
Lexington Reporter,
15 December 1808.

First recorded theatrical
performance in the West,
Mirror (Washington, Ky.),
30 September 1797.
Courtesy of the Rare
Books Collection,
University of Chicago
Library.

ON THURSDAY EVENING, OCTOBER 12th,
Will be performed at the Court House,
BY THE
THEATRICAL SOCIETY
IN THIS TOWN,
The Celebrated Tragedy of
DOUGLAS ;
To which will be added,
The Celebrated Comedy of
LOVE-A-LA-MODE,
And the Musical entertainment of the
PADLOCK.
☞ No Admittance behind the Scenes.
*** *The price of admission this evening will be Half-a-dollar.*
Washington Sept 29, 1796.

THEATRICAL.

WILL be prefented to the public at the Theatre in Lexington, on Thurfday evening the 21ft of May,

THE SCHOOL FOR ARROGANCE;

A Comedy, in Five Acts.

TO WHICH WILL BE ADDED,

THE FARMER;

A Farce, in Two Act .

*** The doors will be opened half after 6 o'Clock, and the curtain will rife half after feven.

†§† Tickets to be had at mr. THOMAS D. OWINGS's Store—*Price Fifty Cents.*

☞ No money received at the door—*No admittance behind the Scenes.*

May 12th. 1801.

First mention of the word *theatre*, *Stewart's Kentucky Herald* (Lexington), 9 May 1801. Courtesy of the Rare Books Collection, University of Chicago Library.

THEATRICAL.

ON Thurfday the 14th of January next will be prefented to the public at the Theatre in Lexington,

THE GAMESTER,

A Tragedy in Five Acts.

To which will be added,

THE DEAD ALIVE,

OR

THE DOUBLE FUNERAL,

A Farce in Three Acts.

TICKETS may be had at either of the Printing Offices in Lexington. Price 50 Cents each.

*** The doors will be opened at 5 o'clock—The curtain will rife at fix.

Unlocated Lexington theatre, *Kentucky Gazette* (Lexington), 1 January 1802. Courtesy of the Rare Books Collection, University of Chicago Library.

Luke Usher's
"The Sign of the Ship,"
Gazette, 26 March 1819.

Blue Beard performance,
Gazette, 17 April 1810.

THEATRE.

On Monday Evening next. May 7, the *MILITARY SOCIETY will perform the*

REVENGE,

A Tragedy in Five Acts, written by Dr Young.

DRAMATIS PERSONÆ,

Don Alonso, (the Spanish General) Mr. Megowan

Don Carlos, (Don Alonzo's friend) Wagnen

Don Alvarez, (A Courtier) C. Bradford

Don Manuel, (Attendant on Don Carlos) Todd

Zanga, (A captive Moor) Marsh.

Leonora, (Alvarez's daughter) Mr. Pindell

Isabella, (the Moor's Mistress) Boggs.

AFTER WHICH WILL BE ADDED THE HUMOROUS FARCE OF

THE VILLAGE LAWYER.

Scout, (the Village Lawyer) Mr. Pindell

Snarl, (a rich Merchant) Wilson

Charles, (Son of Snarl) Todd

Sheep Face, (a Sheep-Stealer) Grant

Justice Mittimus, Comstock.

Constables, Countrymen, &c.

Mrs. Scout, (the Lawyer's wife) Master Boggs

Kate, (wife of Sheep Face) Cock.

A NUMBER OF COMIC SONGS Will be sung during the recess between the Tragedy and Farce.

⁎ Tickets of admission, at 50 Cents each, may be had at the Theatre, and at the Kentucky Gazette office. No money will be received at the door—no admittance for people of colour. Doors to be opened at half past 5 o'clock, and the Curtain to rise at 7 precisely.—Gentlemen are requested not to smoke Segars.

Boxes to be taken on the day of performance.

Every citizen of Lexington must long since have known and lamented its defenceless situation; to raise money by subscription to purchase the necessary arms having failed, the above mean has been resorted to, which only can succeed by the liberal patronage of the citizens. It is hoped, therefore, that even those who have heretofore been opposed to Theatrical exhibitions, will lay by their objections, and instead of considering the manner in which this money is to be obtained, will only view the purposes to which it is to be applied, and the necessity which urged the measure.

The characters, with the names of the performers will be mentioned in the bills of the evening.

Lexington, May 5 h.

First theatre and Old Drury Theatre in Pittsburgh. Courtesy University of Pittsburgh Library.

First recorded cast list in the West, *Gazette*, 1 May 1810.

Jefferson and Blisset in A *Budget of Blunders*.
Courtesy of the Theatre Collection, New York Public Library.

Julia Dean (daughter of Julia Drake).
Courtesy of the Theatre Collection, New York Public Library.

GRAND
CONCERT
OF VOCAL AND INSTRUMENTAL MUSIC,

Under the direction of A. P. HEINRICH,

ASSISTED BY THE PRINCIPAL PROFESSORS AND AMATEURS,

At Mess. KEENE & LANPHEAR's ASSEMBLY ROOM,

On WEDNESDAY EVENING, Nov. 12,

PART 1st.

SIMFONIA con Minuetto	*Beethoven.*	Full Band
GLEE—" When Sappho tuned"		Mess. S. Drake, Blisset, and an
ADAGIO con Sordini e Violino Obligato	*Mozart.*	Full Orchestra. [Amateur
SONG—" The Anchor-Smiths"	*Dibdin.*	Mr. Blisset
DUETTO Concertante, due Violini	*Viotti.*	Mess. S. Drake and Heinrich
CATCH—"Ah! how Sophia," alias "A House on Fire"		Mess. Blisset, Alex. Drake, &
Solo Violino con Variazioni	*Fiorillo.*	Mr. Heinrich [an Amateur
RONDO	*Pleyel.*	Full Band

PART 2d.

GRAND OVERTURE	*Gyrowetz.*	Full Orchestra
SONG—" From blood stain'd plains of glory"		Mr. S. Drake
The celebrated Concerto Violino	*Giornovichi.*	Mr. Heinrich [Amateurs
GHEERFUL GLEE—" Sigh no more, Ladies"		Mess. Blissett, Drake, and
OVERTURE TO LODOISKA, followed by the Queen of Prussia's Waltz, on two Piano Fortes	*Kreutzer & Himmel.*	Mess. Wenzel & Heinrich
COMIC SONG—" The Auctioneer"		Mr. Alexander Drake
CATCH—" It was you that kiss'd the pretty girl"		Mess. S. Drake, Blisset, & A.
FINALE	*Haydn.*	Full Band [Drake

Doors to be opened at 6 o'clock, and performance to commence at half past 6. Tickets of Admission, ONE DOLLAR each, to be had at the several Book-Stores, at Mess. Keene & Lanphear's Bar, and at Mr. Wenzel's Music Store.

Notice from a Lexington newspaper, 12 November 1817, in Heinrich Scrapbook. Courtesy of the Rare Books Collection, Library of Congress.

Notice from a Frankfort newspaper,
26 November 1817, in Heinrich Scrapbook.
Courtesy of the Rare Books Collection,
Library of Congress.

CONCERT
Of Vocal and Instrumental Musi

P. DECLARY & H. M. PENNE

Have the honor to inform the admirers of Harmony, that they will giv
CONCERT ON
Tuesday evening, June 8th, in th

Theatre.

with the assistance of a number of gentlemen Amateurs, and some of t
gentlemen of the Dramatic establishment, who have kindly volunteer
their respective talents.

PART I.

1st.—Overture to Henry 4th—Martini, full Orchestre   leader Mr. *Heinrich.*
2d.—Glee, "When Arthur first at court began;" from the Opera of the Battle of Hexham, Sung by   Messrs. S. *Drake, Alexander & Fisher.*
3d.—Solo, Violin—Variations on Malboro' composed and to be performed by   Mr. *Heinrich.*
4th.—Comic song, 'The Exciseman'   *Alexander.*
5th.—Solo, on the Grand Cabinet Piano, will you come to the Bower with variations,   Mr. *Penner.*

6th—Catch, "Dame Durden,"   S. *Drake, Alexander & F*
7th—Duett, two Violins   *Heinrich & S F*
8th—Song "The old Commodore,"
9th—Solo, Violin—Postillion Waltzes (Concertante) written in imitation of the German Postillion Bugle airs or Post horns, composed and to be executed by   Mr. *He*
10th—Finale Overture to Guy Mannering with favorite Scotch airs, *full Orchestre.*

Between the two parts of the Concert, Mr. Jones of the *Theatre*, will
cite, Dryden's celebrated Ode on

St. Cecelia's day, or Alexander's FEAST.

PART II.

1st—Grand March in the battle of Maringo, *full Orchestre.*
2d—Duett, "All's Well"   S. *Drake & Fisher.*
3d—Plough boy, with variations and accompaniments, by Dusseck, the Piano part to be performed by   *Penner.*
4th—Song, " Be mine dear Maid" from the Opera of Guy Mannering,   Mr. S. *Drake.*
5th—Yankee Doodle varied for the Violin, with the introduction of Hail Columbia, (Violino obligato) composed and to be performed by   Mr. *Heinrich.*

6th—Comic song, "Feyther, mother and Suke"   *Alexan*
7th—Variations on the " Sprig of Shelala" for the Violin   S. *Drak*
8th—Catch, " Old Thomas Day,"
9th—Solo, " Violin,   By an Ama
10th—"Battle of Prague," *full Orchestre,*
11th—Song, "The bald pate Lieutenant,   *Mr. Fis*
12th—Finale, *full Orchestre.*

Doors to open at 7, *Concert* to commence at 8 o'clock.
TICKETS $1, to be had at the Theatre.

Notice from a Louisville newspaper, 8 June 1819, in
Heinrich Scrapbook. Courtesy of the Rare Books Collection,
Library of Congress.

Thomas D. Rice as Jim Crow.
Courtesy of Harper and Brothers, publishers.

bian Inn." They opened their season "for a few nights only" on Monday, May 27, with Mrs. Inchbald's *Animal Magnetism* followed by Colman's *The Wag of Windsor*. Between the comedy and the farce Mrs. Turner recited "Jealousy," and there were comic songs by Williams and by a new actor named James. Cipriani danced a sailor's hornpipe. Performance nights were Mondays and Thursdays, curtain at seven-thirty, and admission price seventy-five cents.[19]

On Saturday, June 3, 1811, the Turners performed *Douglas* and Bickerstaffe's *The Romp, or A Cure for the Spleen*. There were the usual songs between the plays and a fancy dance by Cipriani. Exactly what occurred at the first performance to cause the following announcement in the theatrical notice of the *Western Spy*, June 1, 1811, is not known: "The Ladies and Gentlemen of Cincinnati and its vicinity, are respectfully assured, that efficient means are taken to present any further disturbances. Those who did not receive their tickets at the door will obtain them by applying at the Bar of the Columbian Inn." Mrs. Turner played the leading role of Lady Randolph in *Douglas* and the part of Priscilla Tomboy in *The Romp*. Young Norval was performed by "a gentleman from Lexington" who may have been Kennedy. Turner was having difficulty operating with his few professionals, for on June 8 he announced in the *Western Spy* a word of thanks to "several gentlemen of Cincinnati having kindly condescended to assist in the performance on Monday evening, June 11, 1811." Morton's *Secrets Worth Knowing* headed this attraction; it was followed by the favorite comic opera *The Poor Soldier*.

Using amateurs to fill out the casts, Turner organized two more productions in Cincinnati, publicized in the *Western Spy* on June 15. On Monday, June 17, he produced Thomas Dibdin's musical piece *The Birthday, or Fraternal Discord* and Allingham's farce *The Weathercock, or Love Alone Can Stop Him*. The program included a Polish minuet, songs by Mrs. Turner and Williams, a comic pantomime called *The Clown's Vagaries*,

[19] *Western Spy*, 25 May 1811.

and a masquerade song and dance by Mrs. Turner. It was a full evening of entertainment. According to the *Western Spy*, June 22, the last performance, June 24, was a second showing of *Douglas*, followed by *The Padlock* with a gentleman from Cincinnati playing the leading role of Mungo.

After the Turners had left Cincinnati, the Thespian Corps in that city announced in the July 6 *Western Spy* a performance of *The Poor Gentleman* "in the course of next week." As an addition to the play the amateurs demonstrated a feat that had excelled in both London and Paris, *The Phanthasmagoria*, advertised as "the most scientific, rational, and astounding which modern times have produced." The audience would see, among other things, ghosts and specters floating in the atmosphere. The theatre near the Columbian is not heard from again until 1813.

Since the citizens of Cincinnati did not build a permanent theatre until 1815, the "theatre" used by Turner in 1811 must have been a temporary hall adjoining the Columbian Inn. Helen Langworthy states that on December 15, 1814, at the Columbian a group of citizens organized a stock company for the purpose of building a theatre and that on March 14, 1815, "a small frame building was erected." The Thespians announced that they would use the building for the performance of *John Bull* and *Fortune's Frolic*.[20] When the Turners returned to Cincinnati in 1815, they performed in a temporary theatre erected by amateurs.[21] As late as 1819, Collins and Jones found no permanent theatre in Cincinnati, for they operated in "a room fitted for the purpose of dramatic representation," located on the corner of Columbia and Walnut streets.[22] Thus the theatre occupied by Turner during the summer of 1811 must also have been a room "fitted for the purpose."

The fall season in Lexington was supposed to have opened on Saturday, September 15, 1811, with Colman's *The Poor Gentleman* and an anonymous farce, *The Irishman in Naples*,

---

[20] "The Theatre in the Lower Valley of the Ohio," p. 8.
[21] *Dramatic Life*, p. 117.
[22] *Western Spy*, 19 June 1819.

but because of bad weather the performance was delayed until Saturday, September 21. Douglas's company now operated with the help of Vos, Kennedy, Marsh, Jones, Mrs. Cipriani, and a new actor named Huntington (sometimes spelled Huntingdon) from the New York and Charleston theatres. An actress named Mrs. Jordy played the part of Emily Worthington in *The Poor Gentleman*; her name did not appear in later notices. The Ciprianis had returned to Lexington after a few performances in Cincinnati, and on September 3 Cipriani advertised the reopening of his dancing school; the fee was six dollars per quarter to be paid in advance. In addition to teaching dancing on Mondays and Thursdays from ten to twelve, Cipriani directed a monthly exhibition followed by a ball. The gentlemen of Lexington could also take fencing lessons and exercises in the broadsword from Cipriani. Huntington acted the leading part of Lieutenant Worthington in *The Poor Gentleman* and was praised by a Lexington critic, who wrote that he "was not merely respectable; but by the dignity of deportment as well as by the manner on which he looked and spoke the part he discovered to us that he possessed very superior powers."[23]

From September 21 to November 16—the time of Noble Luke Usher's arrival in Kentucky—Douglas's company presented sixteen plays. They performed two plays with other entertainment almost twice weekly (on Wednesdays and Saturdays) in a newly painted theatre. O'Keeffe's *The Poor Soldier*, new to Lexington audiences, was the only play given a second showing during Douglas's fall season. Eight of the sixteen pieces had never been performed in Kentucky: *The Poor Soldier*; *The Irishman in Naples*; Thomas Otway's *Venice Preserved*; Centlivre's *The Ghost, or The Affrighted Farmer*; Colman's *Who Wants a Guinea?*; Isaac Pocock's *Yes or No, or The Mistakes of a Night*; James Miller's adaptation from Voltaire, *Mahomet, the Imposter*; and Thomas Dibdin's *The Will for the Deed*. The company repeated such standbys as *The Poor Gentleman*, *The Mock Doctor*, *Douglas*, and *The Heir at Law*.[24]

[23] *Gazette*, 10 September, 3 September, 22 October 1811.
[24] *Gazette* and *Reporter*, 21 September to 16 November 1811.

In the September 28 performance of Otway's *Venice Preserved* Huntington played the part of Belvidera, the heroine. John Melish, the English traveler who was wandering through Kentucky during the latter part of September 1811, related that he enjoyed a party at Mr. Brand's house; the group went on to see a play, probably *Venice Preserved*: "We went in a body to the theatre. The performers acted very well, but there was a deficiency of actresses, and one of the men had to play a female character, which did not suit my taste at all. The company are to play here, at Frankfort, and at Louisville."[25] According to Melish, Luke Usher intended to make Louisville the third town in the Kentucky Circuit. Douglas did perform in Frankfort during the 1811-1812 season, but he did not visit Louisville at that time, since he opened in Lexington on February 18, 1812, just after closing in Frankfort on February 13. Dr. John J. Weisert, a Louisville theatrical historian, writes that the Louisville season opened the last half of January 1811.[26] If that is true, Douglas was not there: according to the January 26 *Reporter*, he performed in Lexington on January 26 and 30. The company may have performed briefly in Louisville during the late summer of 1812 when Noble Luke Usher returned from the East with some new players.

During Douglas's fall engagement in 1811 Vos acted the title role in *Adelmorn*, supported by Mrs. Cipriani as Orilla. "A lady, her first on any stage," performed the part of Belinda in *The Ghost*, a notice indicating that Douglas was still having difficulty filling some of the female roles. Cipriani continued to entertain with his hornpipe dance and added an exhibition of broadsword exercises. Kennedy and Huntington sang comic songs; Kennedy also assumed the supporting roles of Old Norval in *Douglas* and Alcanor in *Mahomet*. He was praised by the reviewer for his "power to command and control the passions of his audience."[27] Several casts of players appeared in the Lexington newspapers during the season:

25 Melish, *Travels*, p. 186.
26 John J. Weisert, "Beginnings of the Kentucky Theatre Circuit," *Filson Club History Quarterly*, 34 (July 1960): 273.
27 *Gazette*, 2, 22 October 1811; *Reporter*, 5 October 1811.

The Poor Gentleman

Lt. Worthington	Mr. Huntington
Sir Charles Cropland	Vos
Sir Robert	Douglas
Frederick	Kennedy
Stephen	Marsh
Ollapod	Jones
Emily	Jordy

Adelmorn, the Outlaw

Adelmorn	Vos
Count Ulric	Kennedy
Sigismund	Marsh
Herman	Huntington
Ludewic	Jones
Mugo	Douglas
Orilla	Mrs. Cipriani

Who Wants a Guinea?

Torrent	Douglas
Heartly	Marsh
Sir Larry	Huntington
Barford	Vos
Solomon Grundy	Jones
Andrew	Kennedy
Mrs. Glastonberry	Mrs. Cipriani
Fanny	By a Lady[28]

Thus all appeared to be going well for Douglas as he attempted to reorganize his company in the fall of 1811. His efforts, however, were not appreciated, for by the middle of November Luke Usher had given the management to his son, Noble Luke Usher, who had decided to try his luck with the Kentucky Circuit.

[28] *Gazette*, 10 September, 2 October 1811; *Reporter*, 5 October 1811.

5

The First Western Circuit

Though little is known about Noble Luke Usher before his first recorded performance in Washington, D.C., in 1800, it is certain that he made the rounds of the eastern theatres as a supernumerary before as well as after that year. During the Baltimore season of 1804 he married a Mrs. Snowden, a widow whose maiden name was Harriet L'Estrange. She probably had met Usher as early as 1796, the year of her debut on the Philadelphia stage.

The Ushers acted at the Philadelphia Theatre until 1806, when John Bernard of the Boston Theatre recruited them. Bernard recalled that he added two or three players to his company in 1806: "Among these I must mention Mr. and Mrs. Usher, both clever people, though little known."[1] In 1808 they were performing in Quebec, where Harriet Usher became the lessee of Colonel A. H. Pye's amateur theatre. In the same year Noble Luke Usher attempted to recruit players for a Canadian circuit from Bernard. During the summer of 1809 Bernard visited Montreal and found

a co. playing at Montreal on a sharing scheme, but as deficient in talent as in numbers. Johnson, their acting mgr., I had myself brought on the stage and laid under some obligations. Mills and Usher, the only actors of merit, were both from my own co. and had left Boston, the former a month, the latter a year ago, and with the same object, that of anticipating me in securing the Canadian Circuit, having learned from my own lips that I intended to apply for it on the expiration of the lease of the Boston Theatre. Usher had so far succeeded as to obtain the Quebec House, in the name of his wife for five years.[2]

Between 1809 and their arrival in Lexington in 1811, the Noble Luke Ushers' activity appears to have been limited to Canada, with occasional performances in Boston. Agnes Pye Usher, their first daughter who also became an actress, was born in Canada in 1809; during the same year they performed in *The Robbers* in Boston. In the spring of 1811, before their trip to Kentucky, they played a benefit in Boston for Samuel Drake, the stage manager. Until February 1811 Mrs. Usher was "the darling of the regiment," an amateur stage society connected with the military regiment in Quebec.[3]

The first newspaper notice of Noble Luke Usher's move to Lexington appeared in the *Reporter* on Saturday, November 23, 1811; however, the notice announced "Mr. and Mrs. Usher's second appearance" in Lexington. Their first appearance, if it occurred the Saturday before, was on November 16. A later review in the November 26 *Gazette* showed that Usher's first play was *Hamlet*; the afterpiece was not listed. On November 23 the Ushers performed in O'Keeffe's *Wild Oats, or The Strolling Gentleman* and Arthur Murphy's *Three Weeks after Marriage*. In *Wild Oats* Usher played the leading role of Rover, supported by Mrs. Usher as Lady Amaranth; Mrs. Usher acted the part of Lady Racket in the afterpiece. According to the announcement in the *Reporter* on November 23, the company was to remain only one more week for three performances before opening in Frankfort.

Mr. and Mrs. Noble Luke Usher had made a successful beginning as managers and leading players in the new company. Having worked with both amateur and professional companies, the Ushers made an excellent managing team for the expanding Kentucky Circuit. An unnamed critic hailed their arrival with much flattering praise in the November 26 *Gazette*. After stating

---

[1] *Retrospections of America*, p. 292.
[2] Ibid., pp. 353-54.
[3] "The Theatre in the Lower Valley of the Ohio," chap. 2, note 19.

that they were a "valuable acquisition" to the troupe, he commended Usher for his portrayal of Hamlet, saying that the critics waited until the end of the third act before arriving at the conclusion that he was an actor of "first class" and that he had so much feeling for the role that he was completely identified with it. "His soliloquies were declaimed with proper contemplative deliberation, and although he was, when necessary, sufficiently impassioned, he was exempt from stage rant." Concerning Mrs. Usher, who played Ophelia, the reviewer said that she was much needed in the company since the departure of Mrs. Turner. In the first scene she impressed the audience mainly with her beauty and graceful figure, but in the insane scene her power as an actress triumphed over her physical beauty. She was praised for comedy as well as tragedy, her roles in *Wild Oats* and *Three Weeks after Marriage* being enthusiastically received.

On November 27 Kotzebue's *Menschenhass und Reue,* known as *The Stranger,* gave the Ushers an opportunity to display their emotional range. The November 26 *Gazette* announced that Usher would play the Stranger to his wife's Mrs. Haller, Kennedy would provide comic relief after the drama with the comic song "Murder in Irish," and *The Mock Doctor* would bring the entertainment to a close.

For the last performance of the season on Saturday, November 30, 1811, announced in the *Reporter* of the same day, Usher presented Cumberland's *The Wheel of Fortune* and Allingham's *Fortune's Frolic.* The Ushers played the leading roles of Penruddock and Emily Tempest in Cumberland's play. A notice in the *Gazette* of December 3, 1811, thanked the citizens of Lexington for their liberal support of the theatre and announced that the company would be performing in Frankfort for two months. Cipriani announced that he would continue with his dancing school on his return from Frankfort.

Usher had chosen some of the best-liked plays of the period for his opening engagement in Lexington. *The Stranger* was one of the most successful sentimental pieces performed during the first part of the nineteenth century. First acted at Drury

Lane in 1798, it drew such tremendous responses from the audiences that several adaptations from the German found their way to the English stage. Though Benjamin Thompson's version was the most popular, Cumberland and Dunlap also wrote successful adaptations. Kotzebue's treatment of an unfaithful wife who is forgiven by her husband greatly appealed to nineteenth-century audiences. O'Keeffe's *Wild Oats* presents a character named Rover who turns out to be the missing son of an aristocratic gentleman. The play had its first American production in 1793 and "proved one of the most successful comedies of the epoch."[4] Cumberland's more serious play, *The Wheel of Fortune*, has another mistaken-identity plot, this one involving Penruddock's revenge on the man who turns out to be the son of the woman he loves.

An interesting announcement appeared in the *Gazette* on Tuesday, December 3, 1811, the same day Usher announced his move to Frankfort. It was written by Richard Jones, the company's scenic artist, and it was addressed to "an enlightened and liberal public." After thanking the patrons of Lexington and Frankfort, Jones called his employer, Luke Usher, "tyrannical and avaricious." He complained of many occasions of "bullying and dishonest" treatment given him by Usher. Despite excellent audiences and profits of $400.00, Jones, after much hard work painting scenery, had received only $21.25, and he did not have enough money to make the trip to Frankfort for the engagement there. He also complained that the members of the company had to pay their own expenses while most of the profits went to the managers and that Luke Usher, like the "Tyrant Richard," had no more need for him since the return of Noble Luke Usher, who now performed all of Jones's roles.

In the December 24, 1811, *Gazette* Luke Usher replied to Jones's letter, claiming that Jones's contract stipulated that Jones would receive an extra benefit in return for his scene-painting duties. Usher stated that at the end of the first two weeks of the season the theatre had taken in $365.00; however, since

[4] G. C. Seilhamer, *The History of the American Theatre*, 3 vols. (Philadelphia, 1891), 1: 69.

he could not estimate what the rest of the season would earn, he had agreed with Douglas and Kennedy that they would draw smaller salaries until the end of the engagement, and he had agreed with Jones that he would draw $12.00 per week, "about the amount of a comedian's salary." Usher stated that he had paid Jones $24.00 for two weeks' work but that Jones had demanded more. He concluded by saying that the company was indebted to him for the sum of $407.27 at the time of the Frankfort engagement and that Jones owed $142.67 of that amount.

That the first western circuit managed to draw good audiences and to make money is evident from Jones's complaint. The actors, however, were being paid as little as possible by the "tyrannical" Luke Usher, whose eye for business was a cause of dissension throughout the period. His penurious tactics had probably caused the Turners and the Ciprianis to leave the company in 1811, and in 1815 William Turner sued Usher for failure to comply with an agreement concerning the Kentucky Circuit management. In fact, Usher was involved in thirteen legal actions from 1815 to 1818; eventually his failure to pay the mortgage on his theatre building in 1825 resulted in its sale at public auction.[5]

At least three persons named Jones performed in the western theatres before 1820. Richard Jones, or John R. Jones, was the scene designer and actor whose name first occurs in Douglas's company in Lexington during the 1810 engagement. After his disagreement with Usher in December 1811 Jones left Lexington for Pittsburgh and later New Orleans, where his name appeared in 1817 as scene designer in an amateur production at the newly built Olympic Circus.[6] As late as 1835, according to Ludlow, Richard Jones was a performer and scene designer in the Mobile Theatre. Ludlow also speaks of a Samuel P. Jones, a former printer, who became "stage-mad" and joined him in St. Louis in 1819.[7] Samuel Jones appeared as a "heavy" actor in

[5] *Reporter,* 5 September 1825.
[6] Nellie Smither, A *History of the English Theatre in New Orleans* (New York, 1967), p. 13.
[7] *Dramatic Life,* pp. 434, 182.

several of Ludlow's western theatrical enterprises from 1819 to 1828. William Jones, an excellent actor and manager, was the most important Jones to appear on the early western stage. Before joining an actor named Collins to manage the Cincinnati Theatre in 1820, William Jones had performed in Lexington and many other western and southern towns.

Granting that Frankfort had sponsored stage activity as early as 1807 and had witnessed a short professional season when Douglas played there in 1810-1811, the capital city officially entered the Kentucky Circuit with the Noble Luke Ushers' opening of the Frankfort Theatre in 1811-1812. It was a lengthy, successful engagement beginning on December 7 and ending on February 13. Included in the first *Palladium* notice, November 22, 1811, was an announcement taken from the *Gazette* concerning the Ushers' arrival in Lexington:

The friends of the drama will be pleased to learn that the arrival of Mr. and Mrs. Usher, of the Boston and Quebec Theatres, is momently expected in this place. The Theatrical Corps at present here, tho highly respectable, is deficient in numbers— and has consequently appeared to great disadvantage and laboured under much inconvenience in many instances. It is therefore with pleasure stated that the determination of the friends of Theatrical exhibitions to place the establishment here of equal rank with those of the Atlantic cities, together with the exertions of the managers to effect this object, has been thus far successful; and we look forward to an early period of time, when the Lexington Theatre will assume a standing that will do credit to the taste, judgement and spirit of its citizens. The zeal and perseverance of those engaged in erecting and fostering the Kentucky stage, do them individually much credit, and will no doubt receive a just applause and support— difficulties have been conquered and prejudice surmounted— nothing then remains to ensure a final accomplishment of the laudable undertaking but *good management and proper regulation*. . . . The "Critique" assigns Mr. Usher an eminent station in tragedy. Cooke and Cooper alone outrank him. Mrs. Usher also has been the subject of many rich encomiums—a combination of powers being ascribed to her.

The newspapers failed to announce the names of the first plays given during this Frankfort engagement. The *Palladium* announced on Friday, November 22, that Frankfort's new theatre would be ready for the visiting company from Lexington at the opening of the General Assembly. The theatre was described as "equal, if not superior to any in the Western Country" in size, convenience and elegance. Though the newspapers failed to give its location, later information reveals that it was a second-floor theatre in a three-story building located on the southeast corner of Broadway and St. Clair streets (the site now occupied by Horn's Drug Store), opposite the old Capitol. The building was owned by an Englishman named Barstow who operated a store on the ground floor.[8] Facing north on Broadway, the building measured fifty-eight feet, four inches; it had a depth on St. Clair Street of forty-two feet, six inches.[9] These dimensions indicate that the Frankfort Theatre was small, but later descriptions show that it had a pit, boxes, a gallery, and a bar.[10] Both Melish's account and later newspaper accounts confirm that the theatre was built by citizen subscription to "counteract an evident propensity for gaming and other dissipations which had become alarming to the hopes and prospects of many of our citizens."[11]

Noble Luke Usher's second production in Frankfort, on Monday, December 9, 1811, was Shakespeare's *Hamlet*, followed by the farce *Three Weeks after Marriage*. The cast of the plays, one of the few listings in the Frankfort newspapers during this season, was given in the *American Republic* on Friday, December 6, 1811:

Hamlet, Prince of Denmark

Hamlet	Mr. Usher
King	Mr. Marsh
Horatio	Mr. Vos

[8] Bayliss E. Hardin, "Notes from Frankfort Newspapers" (manuscript, Kentucky Historical Society, Frankfort).
[9] Franklin County Deed Book 1 (Frankfort, Ky.), p. 354.
[10] *Argus of Western America*, 20 November 1818.
[11] *Commentator*, 29 January 1819.

Laertes	Mr. Kennedy
Ghost	Mr. Huntington
Guildenstern	Mr. Cipriani
Polonius	Mr. Douglass
Ophelia	Mrs. Usher
Gertrude	Mrs. Cipriani
Player Queen	Mrs. Vos

Three Weeks after Marriage

Sir Charles Racket	Mr. Kennedy
Drugget	Mr. Douglass
Footman	Mr. Cipriani
Lady Racket	Mrs. Usher
Mrs. Drugget	Mrs. Cipriani
Dimity	Mrs. Vos

The *American Republic* also informed the public that the theatre opened at five-thirty for a six o'clock performance. Boxes, selling for one dollar, half price for parties with children, were "taken" by Mr. Usher from nine until one o'clock at the theatre. Usher performed three times weekly, on Monday, Wednesday, and Friday, "excepting week of Dancing Assemblies."

In fourteen announced performances (there were others not advertised) Usher gave the Frankfort audiences twenty-eight plays and the usual songs, dances, and recitations. He offered second showings of *Catherine and Petruchio, Macbeth, Pizarro, Tekeli, The Stranger*, and *Venice Preserved*, probably the most popular plays of the season. All the plays were new to Frankfort audiences, but only four were first showings in Kentucky: Colman's *The Mountaineers, or Love and Madness*, a farce of intrigue taken from Cervantes's *Don Quixote*; Colman's *Blue Devils*, a love farce borrowed from a French play by Joseph Patrat; Bickerstaffe's *The Romp*, an alteration of his *Love in the City* (a musical entertainment in two acts); and Holcroft's *The Road to Ruin*, another sentimental piece showing the evils of gambling. None of these new offerings was repeated. *Love-a-la-Mode, The Spoiled Child*, and *The Village Lawyer* continued to serve as stock pieces.

Newspaper notices in Frankfort were brief, listing the names of the plays, the dates, and occasionally an abbreviated cast. On December 13, 1811, the *American Republic* announced that the Frankfort Theatre had opened on December 7 and that three plays had been produced in the new theatre. The article congratulated the company on the successful opening engagement and thanked them for helping to alleviate gambling during the winter months. During the engagement Kennedy and Mrs. Usher played the leading roles of Durimel and Bertha in *Point of Honor* and starred as Lovell and Kitty in the afterpiece, *High Life below Stairs*. Cipriani danced his hornpipe after the play. The *American Republic*'s notice of *Venice Preserved* on December 27, 1811, stated that repeated calls for comic songs by the audience caused disorder in the theatre and that the entertainment listed in the bills should not be superseded by audience requests. According to the January 1, 1812, *Palladium*, the performance of *Catherine and Petruchio* featured as an afterpiece a dazzling spectacle: a Corinthian arch, supported by four columns, dedicated to Washington and other historical figures. The arch, inscribed with the names of the states, exhibited the motto "We Laud the Men Who Saved the States." All of this concluded with a chorus of "Hail Columbia." Between the drama and the spectacle the audience heard recitations, "Seven Ages of Man," "Alonzo and Imogene," and a parody, "Giles Jolly the Grave and the Brown Sally Green." Along with the *Tekeli* notice of January 27, 1812, the *American Republic* announced a performance of "Feats of Horsemanship" by a man named Rickets to be given the next day at three o'clock. One short review of *The Stranger* appeared in the *Palladium* on February 12, 1812. After praising Mrs. Usher's interpretation of Mrs. Haller, the leading role, the critic said that *"The Stranger* seized hold on the feelings of the spectators, and irresistibly carried them away, until they were relieved by a universal shower of tears." The same review stated that the audience for the last performance of *Tekeli* would be a "thin house" since the legislature was no longer in session.

During the more than two-month engagement in Frankfort, Lexington had three performances in a place advertised as the New Theatre, or Traveller's Hall Revived. (Traveller's Hall, mentioned earlier as the location of various entertainments, was located on the public square directly opposite the north-west front of the courthouse.) The first production, *The Mountaineers* and *High Life below Stairs*, took place on Wednesday, January 1, 1812; the second, *Macbeth* and *Sprigs of Laurel*, on Saturday, January 4; and the third, *Pizarro*, on Saturday, January 18.[12]

The newspapers offered little information about these productions except that they were to have "new scenery, dresses and decorations" and that tickets would cost fifty cents. Usher was performing these same plays in Frankfort during the time they were advertised in Lexington; he and his company may have returned to Lexington to assist amateurs with performances there. He could not, however, have helped with the January 1 production in Lexington of *The Mountaineers*, since he was performing *Catherine and Petruchio* on the same date in Frankfort. Furthermore, it is doubtful that he would have assisted in the other productions without advertising the names of his players. The fifty-cent ticket price characterizes the Lexington productions as amateurish, yet three productions of five plays given in little more than two weeks would have been difficult for amateurs to manage without professional help.

Returning to Lexington on Tuesday, February 18, 1812, Usher presented *Othello* and *Blue Devils*. Mrs. Usher acted Desdemona to her husband's Othello. A new actor from Philadelphia named Cross performed Iago; and Huntington, Kennedy, Douglas, and Mrs. Cipriani played the roles of Cassio, Roderigo, Brabantio, and Emilia, respectively.[13] Cross must have been filling in for Vos for this one performance since Cross's name does not appear again.

Usher gave Lexington audiences thirteen productions from February 18 through April 21, 1812. Each performance featured two plays and the usual songs and recitations. Larger crowds must have been attending the theatre, for one announcement in

[12] *Reporter*, 31 December 1811, 4, 14 January 1812.
[13] *Gazette*, 18 February 1812.

the *Gazette* explained that additional doors had been built to accommodate the public. The season saw repeat performances of such popular plays as *Blue Devils, The Review, The Spoiled Child,* and *Pizarro* (which was shown three times). Seldom did the newspaper print the entire casts, but occasionally the important roles of a popular piece such as *Pizarro* found their way to the press. In *Pizarro* the Ushers took the leading roles of Rolla and Cora, Vos played Pizarro, and Mrs. Cipriani performed Elvira. Between the drama and the farce Mrs. Usher recited "Seven Ages of Woman" and Mrs. Cipriani replied with "Seven Ages of Man." Other between-the-plays entertainment came from Huntington, who presented two satirical law cases, Kennedy, who repeated the comic song "Murder in Irish," and Usher, who recited "Alonzo and Imogene."[14] The audience received its seventy-five cents' worth.

The new plays of the spring season show, with the exception of *Othello,* a preponderance of trite, sentimental comedies and melodramatic, spectacular serious plays. Only such old favorites as *The Romp, The Review,* and *Blue Devils* had repeat performances during the season. The serious dramas included *The Death of André,* William Dunlap's tragedy of an American Revolutionary spy, one of the earliest American plays to be performed in the West; *Rudolphe, or The Robber of Calabria,* a spectacular melodrama by John Turnbull; *Zara,* an adaptation from Voltaire's sentimental tragedy by Aaron Hill; and *De Montfort,* Joanne Baille's melodramatic polemic on hate. On the lighter side, Colman, the most popular dramatist thus far in the West, was represented by *The Battle of Hexam,* a three-act, sentimental hodge-podge of love and adventure. John Burgoyne's *The Maid of the Oaks,* a musical piece with the usual mistaken identity mixup, and John O'Keeffe's *The Prisoner at Large,* one of a long list of farcical pieces using trite complications between servants and masters, were also performed.

Most of the so-called tragedies of the period were little more than declamatory, melodramatic, sentimental displays. *Zara,* written in 1736 and first starring Mrs. Cibber in the title role, is a

---

[14] *Reporter,* 17 March 1812.

good example of this popular style. Zara is a slave to the sultan but is in love with a French officer who has vowed to save her from a fate worse than death. She makes the following valiant confession of Christianity at the end of the play:

ZARA: O! My Father! Dear author of my life!
Inform me, teach me, what thou'd my Duty do?
LUSIGNAN: By one short Word,
To dry up all my tears,
And make life Welcome,
Say, thou art a Christian—
ZARA: Sir—I am a Christian.
LUSIGNAN: Receive her, gracious Heaven!
and bless her for it.
(Osman stabs Zara and kills self).

The best comedies as well as the serious pieces had a streak of sentiment running through them. Sentimental writing became such a stereotyped dramatic technique that some of the better playwrights of the period attempted, though with little success, to break the pattern. Although Sheridan used sentiment in his plays, he criticized its slavish employment in a bit of dialogue in his famous *School for Scandal*:

OLIVER: 'Tis edification to hear him
converse; he professes the
noblest sentiments.
PETER: Oh, plague of his sentiments!
If he salutes me with a scrap
of morality in his mouth, I
shall be sick directly.

The professional season closed on Saturday, April 25, with a production of *Zara* and *Children in the Wood*. Luke Usher donated his theatre to the Thespians for a production on May 30, 1812, of Colman's popular farce *John Bull, or The Englishman's Fireside* and Oulton's musical farce *The Sixty-Third Letter*. The proceeds from the performance went to the Lexington Volunteers Company of Light Infantry to purchase arms, ammunition, and camp equipment for the march to Canada. The

Thespian Volunteers were busy again on Thursday, June 11, with a production of Frederick Reynolds's *The Blind Bargain, or Hear It Out,* another farcical comedy. The afterpiece was the often played comedy *The Spoiled Child.* These plays were advertised as benefit productions for Mrs. Usher and Mrs. Cipriani.[15]

On Wednesday, August 5, 1812, the *Palladium* announced the arrival in Frankfort of Noble Luke Usher with "some performers from the Eastward." The Frankfort Theatre, according to the same notice, was to have opened on Monday, August 10, for a few nights. The only other newspaper information concerning that engagement, however, appeared in the *Palladium* on Wednesday, August 19, the "last night," when the company performed Goldsmith's *She Stoops to Conquer* and Robert Jephson's farce *Two Strings to Your Bow, or The Servant of Two Masters.* Why Usher had planned an engagement in Frankfort at this time is not known. Although his name is mentioned in the Frankfort announcement, Noble Luke Usher and his wife are not listed in the Kentucky Circuit theatrical notices again until a *Gazette* announcement of July 13, 1813. Perhaps they found a profitable engagement in the East. Francis Wemyss's *Chronology* records that Noble Luke Usher established the theatre in Norfolk, Virginia, in 1812.[16] Usher may have refused to continue with the management of the Kentucky Circuit until Luke Usher relinquished the management of the theatre and rented it to the company, an action recorded in the June 5, 1813, *Reporter.*

On August 1, 1812, the *Reporter* advertised that the theatre in Lexington would open on that date for three nights only with Charles Kemble's adaptation from the French, *Point of Honor, or A School for Soldiers* and the old favorite *The Midnight Hour.* Either this production failed to take place or was not further advertised, for no other theatrical notice appeared in Lexington until September 29. Since Usher's company did not

---

15 *Gazette,* 26 May, 11 June 1812.
16 *Chronology of the American Stage,* p. 12.

perform again in Lexington until October 1, they may have been engaged in Louisville after the last Frankfort performance on August 19; however, none of the Louisville newspapers recorded performances at this time.

In addition to losing the Noble Luke Ushers in 1812, the company was without the services of Vos, who was last heard from in an announcement in the *Gazette* on June 9, 1812. The advertisement stated that John H. Vos was doing house painting and was also painting carriages at the brick house below the Branch Bank in Lexington. Vos is not heard from again until June 13, 1814, when he again advertised in Lexington his house, sign, and coach painting business.

Two of Usher's recruits, John Vaughan and Mrs. Doige, arrived from Boston in time to star in *Point of Honor*, Vaughan playing Durimel and Mrs. Doige supporting him as Bertha. Another Boston actor, George Bland, had joined the company by September 29. Later in the season three other strolling actors, Mr. and Mrs. Thornton and Webster, acted with the company for a short period. Bland, who began acting in America under the name of Wilson, was the brother of the celebrated English actress Mrs. Jordan. His wife, Maria Theresa Romanzini, was a well-known dancer and ballad singer at Drury Lane. Dunlap records that Bland made his American debut in New York in 1802 under the name of Wilson, acting the role of Frank Oatland in the comedy *A Cure for the Heart Ache*. "He proved to be a man of indifferent character but possessed talents for the stage. He afterwards was very serviceable in getting up the opera of *Blue Beard*, and played Shakabac with effect."[17] Ludlow speaks of meeting Bland during a Pittsburgh engagement in 1815 when Bland performed for a few times with Samuel Drake's company. Bland probably encountered Noble Luke Usher in Boston or New York in 1812 and was persuaded to join the players in Kentucky. Ludlow calls him an actor "who had seen better days, and possessed

[17] William Dunlap, *The History of the American Theatre* (New York, 1832), p. 294.

at some previous time greater vocal power than he then [1815] manifested." During the Pittsburgh engagement Bland left the company and was not heard of again until many years later when Ludlow found him in Mississippi living among the Choctaw and Chickasaw Indians.[18] Little is known about the other actors who joined Usher later in the summer of 1812. John Vaughan's name occurs frequently in Ludlow's account, along with Vaughan's younger brother, Henry; both joined Drake in Frankfort during the 1815–1816 engagement. Ludlow took the Vaughans with him on his tour through the South in 1817.

The fall and winter engagement in Lexington was erratic, with performances occurring on different nights of the week from October 1 through December 5. No performances took place from October 13 to November 3 and from November 5 to November 25. Despite the apparently disorganized schedule, the troupe without the leadership of the Ushers managed to present nineteen plays, ten of which were new to Kentucky audiences, on nine different evenings.

Shakespeare's *The Merchant of Venice*, performed on Saturday, November 28, was the sixth Shakespearean play to be shown in Kentucky, including Garrick's version of *The Taming of the Shrew*. *Macbeth*, with four performances, was the most popular Shakespearean drama thus far; *Catherine and Petruchio* and *Othello* had three performances each, and *Romeo and Juliet, Henry IV*, and *The Merchant of Venice* each had one showing, making a total of thirteen performances of Shakespeare. After 1812 only Colman was more popular than Shakespeare.

Nathaniel Lee's *The Rival Queens, or Alexander the Great*, one of the better heroic dramas of the Restoration period, provided the occasion for the scene designer to construct a triumphal entry of Alexander into Babylon. The entry had the support of a "Grand Chorus" singing "See the Conquering Hero Come." A "Grand Banquet" followed in act four.[19] Col-

[18] *Dramatic Life*, pp. 70-71.
[19] *Gazette*, 6 October 1812.

man's *Inkle and Yarico*, a popular operatic play in three acts, was one of the many musical pieces presented to Lexington audiences in 1812 before the troupe moved to Frankfort. This musical extravaganza, full of pathos, relates the travels of Inkle in America while on his way to marry a princess in Barbados. Again the scene designer was challenged to display colorful settings this time representing the New World. The newspapers announced several other new musical plays, both light and serious: *The Purse, or The American Tar*, a one-act musical farce by J. D. Cross; *The Adopted Child, or Milford Castle*, a Gothic musical melodrama by Samuel Birch; and *The Bee Hive, or Lots of Confusion*, a musical farce with "lots of confusion" by John Millingen.

Aside from conventional farces, such as Hannah Cowley's *Who's the Dupe? or The Prize for Literature*, and melodramas of intrigue, such as William Dimond's *The Doubtful Son, or Secrets of a Palace*, the company presented John Tobin's *The Honeymoon*, a popular blank verse comedy which had had a successful opening at Drury Lane in 1805. Lexington audiences also saw revivals of *The Jew, Animal Magnetism, The Mountaineers, Blue Beard, The Poor Soldier, The Rivals, The Padlock*, and *The Waterman*.[20]

On Monday, November 23, a strolling singer named Webster performed a musical entertainment, "The Wandering Melodist," in Postlethwait's Inn ballroom. For the price of seventy-five cents the audience could hear Webster sing "Sally Roy," "Fair Ellen, Faithless Emma," and other songs. After his second performance Webster joined the company at the theatre, where he assisted with the productions of *The Rivals* and *The Padlock*, performing the role of Leander in the latter piece. On Saturday, November 28, he sang "The Thorn" and "The Willow" during the performance of *The Merchant of Venice*; just how these songs were fitted into the play is not known. He also assisted in some way with the performance on December 1 of *Inkle and Yarico, The Bee Hive*, and *The Waterman*. For his final appearance in Lexington on December

20 Ibid., 1 October 1812; *Reporter*, 5 December 1812.

5, 1812, he sang "Come Take the Harp," "Down in the Valley," and "The Exile of Erin." The newspapers announced these songs along with the performances of *The Honeymoon* and *The Faithful Irishman, or Honest Thieves.*[21] *The Faithful Irishman* is one of several farcial adaptations of *The Committee* by Robert Howard.

On Saturday, December 12, 1812, Webster thanked the people of Lexington for supporting his performances and announced that he would take a benefit in Frankfort on Wednesday, January 20, 1813. He moved to Frankfort with the company and performed as a singer in several of the performances. Concerning Webster's popularity in Frankfort, the following complaint to Luke Usher appeared in the December 9 *Palladium:* "Why does Usher charge the people of Frankfort $1.00 and the people of Lexington (22 miles) 75¢? Why not a song from the great Mr. Webster?"

Not much is known about Webster before his arrival in Lexington during the 1812–1813 season. On October 12, 1812, just before his arrival in Kentucky, he performed for two nights in Pittsburgh in a large room belonging to L. Porter. His program of songs was advertised as "Variety, or The Songster's Jubilee." The newspaper notice also stated that Webster had performed in the theatres of London, Dublin, Edinburgh, Philadelphia, and Baltimore.[22] His name first appeared in New York on July 3, 1807, when he performed an evening of songs at the assembly room of the City Hotel. Apparently this was not his American debut, for his advertisement stated that he had earlier performed in Philadelphia.[23] After leaving Kentucky, Webster performed in Cincinnati on October 22 and November 1, 1813. The October 22 *Western Spy* announced his appearance at the assembly room of the Columbian Inn, where he sang "Sally Roy," "Fair Ellen," "The Willow," and "Paddy in a Pucker." Odell believes that "Webster was

[21] *Reporter*, 21 November, 5 December 1812.
[22] "Trends in Commercial Entertainment," p. 121.
[23] George C. D. Odell, *Annals of the New York Stage*, vol. 2 (New York, 1927), p. 288.

probably a good singer,"[24] and Wemyss, speaking of Webster's performance in Philadelphia in 1816, says that he "possessed a tolerable and well-cultivated voice."[25]

In addition to the announced songs by Webster during the 1812 Lexington season, Usher's regular actors entertained with songs. The October 22 *Reporter* announced that during the performance of *The Mountaineers* Mrs. Cipriani sang "When the Hollow Drum"; she was joined by Bland for a rendition of "O! Happy Tawney Moor." Kennedy, Bland, and Douglas presented "You High Born Spanish Nobleman," and Kennedy sang a solo called "At Sixteen Years Old." The music concluded with a duet by Bland and Mrs. Cipriani, "The Way Worn Traveller."

Before Webster's arrival Bland had received the company's only critical reviews. The *Gazette*, October 6, 1812, praised his comic powers in his portrayal of Jabel in *The Jew*: "He is unquestionably the best low comedian we have seen in the western world. The Co. at this time is very respectable, and tho' with regret I saw thin houses last week, I doubt not I shall with pleasure shortly witness it crowded when our brave sons of freedom shall return Victorious."

On December 9 the company returned to Frankfort for a few performances, opening with Tobin's *The Honeymoon* and the farce *The Village Lawyer*. Performing once a week, on Wednesdays, the company produced *The Rivals, Sprigs of Laurel, Pizarro, Miss in Her Teens, Blue Beard,* and *The Romp*.[26] An interesting announcement in the *Palladium* on December 16 describes a full-dress ball for the patrons of the theatre on the night of December 23. The pit was converted into a dancing area, and the actors planned to appear in costume, representing characters from the various plays presented during the season. Frankfort citizens who desired to participate in the dancing were warned to "come in shoes," probably a suggestion that they wear dancing shoes. Tickets at the price of $1.50, or $1.00

[24] Ibid.
[25] *Chronology of the American Stage*, p. 147.
[26] *Palladium*, 9, 16 December 1812, 20, 27 January 1813.

for the balcony, could be purchased from "Captain Weisiger and of Messrs. Vaughan at Dr. Newberry." The Frankfort season closed after the performance on January 27, 1813. Garrick's *Miss in Her Teens*, a popular farce of intrigue, was the only new play of the season.

One interesting bit of information about the Frankfort Theatre in 1813 concerns the January 22 defeat and massacre of the Kentucky Volunteers at River Raisin: "At the commencement of the War of 1812, . . . The bloody tragedy of Raisin had been enacted. We remember *that well*. We were but a small boy at the time, and had made our way into the theatre upon a much prized half price ticket. Governor Shelby and family were in the boxes, when an express, all besmattered with mud, made his appearance, and whispered in the ear of the Governor. He arose and left the house. Immediately the news spread over the audience that the detachment was cut to pieces."[27] G. Glenn Clift, quoting from a manuscript in the Kentucky Historical Society, describes the three-story theatre building as having a narrow stairway leading to the second-floor auditorium. Had a fire broken out during the performance, the audience would have had difficulty in escaping. Despite its crude structure, however, the theatre had a long history as a place of theatrical entertainment. Many favorite stars such as the elder Booth and Mrs. Alexander Drake visited it in later years. About 1854 the building did burn.[28]

With the exception of one Louisville theatrical notice, Usher's company was not heard from again in 1813 until the opening of their Lexington season in April. The *Western Courier*, a Louisville newspaper, advertised on Tuesday, March 22, 1813, a benefit performance of *Pizarro* and *Raising the Wind* for Thornton, an actor who had recently joined Usher's troupe. Although this is the only notice of the 1813 Louisville engagement, it reveals that the Lexington actors visited Louisville for at least a part of the period from March 26 to May 19, 1813.

[27] Quoted in Orlando Brown, "The Governors of Kentucky," *Register of the Kentucky Historical Society* 49 (April 1951): 96.
[28] Ibid., note 13.

After an absence of seven months, the longest period of absence since the opening of the Lexington Theatre, Usher's company returned to Lexington on Wednesday, May 19, 1813, with a new play, William Dimond's *The Foundling of the Forest*, announced in the May 18 *Gazette*. The season was a long one, running through November 13, with performances occurring mainly on Wednesdays and occasionally on Saturdays. The doors of the theatre now opened at seven o'clock for an eight o'clock performance, the latest performance hour thus far announced. Seats in both the pit and the boxes cost one dollar, and gallery seats were fifty cents.

In July 1813 Usher's company was strengthened by the return of the Turners from Cincinnati and Pittsburgh. Since the last amateur production in Cincinnati on July 6, 1811, drama in that city had been unannounced until Saturday, March 27, 1813, when the *Western Spy* announced that the theatre on Broadway would be used for a public benefit on Monday, March 30. For fifty cents Cincinnati audiences could witness *The Execution, or Troublesome Friendship* and *The Battle of Tippecanoe*. Songs, a war dance, and an epilogue ended the performance. Two other performances took place in Cincinnati in 1813. The first, on July 3, was announced in the July 3 *Western Spy* as a "Naval Representation" in anticipation of the July 4 celebration; it was followed by the afterpiece *Yankee Chronology*. The second performance was Webster's concert of October 24. No other drama notices appeared in the Cincinnati newspapers until 1815, when the Turners came back.

Mr. and Mrs. Noble Luke Usher returned to Lexington to manage thirty-eight plays on twenty-one evenings from May 19 through November 13, 1813. Only four of the plays had repeat performances, and three of these were new to the company. Lexington audiences saw seventeen new dramas during this spring and fall engagement, the longest and most successful season ever presented in the West. Except for the announcement of benefit performances, the notices gave little information concerning the performers or their roles in the plays. Mrs. Cipriani and Mrs. Thornton did a fancy dance following the performance of *The Busy Body*, and Mrs. Thornton also did a fancy dance after *The Stranger;* during the same evening Mrs. Usher sang "Barnyard." Vaughan and Bland continued to sing between plays, and one critic commented upon Bland's "incomparable talents." Mrs. Usher is mentioned in connection with the company, but Mrs. Turner played the leading roles in both *Romeo and Juliet* and *Jane Shore.* (Mrs. Usher died the following March and may have been too ill to perform during this season.) On Saturday, November 6, after the performance of *The Widow of Malabar*, Vaughan and Gaston presented what the *Reporter* of the same date called a "grand display of The Brilliant Victory gained by Commodore Perry over the British squadron on Lake Erie." Mrs. Turner acted with Usher's company for only four nights, beginning on July 3, 1813, in *Jane Shore* and *The Spoiled Child;* her last performance in *Romeo and Juliet* took place on Saturday, July 17, when she also gave a farewell address to the patrons of the drama. The Turners were not heard from again in Kentucky until 1815.

Musical plays, both light and serious, continued to be in high favor during this season in Lexington. William Dimond's *The Foundling of the Forest*, a sentimental tale of villainy, uses songs and instrumental music to heighten the intrigue. John O'Keeffe's popular *Highland Reel*, another of his comic operas, is a musical hodge-podge of mistaken identity. Carlo Delpini's *Don Juan, or The Libertine Destroyed* is a tragic pantomime with music by Cristoph Willibald Gluck.[29] Spanish intrigue, one of the popular plot scources of the period, appeared again with Colman's comic opera *The Spanish Barber*, based on Beaumarchais's *The Barber of Seville.* Sheridan's farce *St. Patrick's Day, or The Scheming Lieutenant* contained the usual love and marriage plot enacted by such characters as Dr. Rosy, Sergeant Trounce, Corporal Flint, and Bridget Credulous.

The season had its share of heroic, spectacular melodramas. A Norman invasion is the scene for Cumberland's *The*

---

[29] Allardyce Nicoll, *A History of English Drama, 1660–1900* (Cambridge, 1955), vol. 3, *1750–1800*, p. 253.

Carmelite, a heroic piece in verse; *The Man of Fortitude, or The Robber Spectre,* an adaptation by Dunlap, is a Gothic spectacle dealing with ghosts and villainous intrigues; James Boaden's *Fontainville Forest,* based on Mrs. Radcliffe's *Romance of the Forest,* follows the same Gothic pattern executed with the help of a heroine with the romantic name of Adeline.

Domestic melodrama, spectacular and poetic, headed the bills, with titles such as *Bunker Hill* and *The Widow of Malabar. Bunker Hill,* John Burk's spectacle of the American Revolution, was one of the few early American plays to be performed in the West. In *The Widow of Malabar,* Mariana Starke's poetic melodrama set before the exotic pagoda of Eswara, a widow is to die on a pyre with her slain husband; this play is an adaptation from A. M. Lemierre's *La Veuve de Malabar.*[30] Another domestic piece, advertised as a five-act comedy called *Man and Wife, or More Secrets Than One,* is, as the title shows, a sentimental piece dealing with marriage problems.

Comic relief was added by Usher with *Tit for Tat, or Natural Deception,* a farcical comedy by Joseph Atkinson; *The Day after the Wedding, or A Wife's First Lesson,* a farcical comedy of manners by Marie Therese de Camp, the wife of Charles Kemble; and *Blind Geladin, or How to Die for Love,* a farcical comedy by Kotzebue dealing with the wornout plot of a girl forced to choose between two prospective husbands. Usher repeated his old drawing-card pieces such as *The Stranger, Blue Devils, Abaellino, The Padlock, The Mountaineers, The Busy Body, Sprigs of Laurel, The Road to Ruin, Who's the Dupe?* and *Romeo and Juliet.* An anonymous comedy, *The Soldier's Benefit, or An Example to Volunteers,* performed on June 29, served as Mrs. Doige's benefit. A play called *The Virgin of the Sun,* another title for the first part of *Pizarro* as adapted by Dunlap from Kotzebue, was produced on May 26.[31]

There is no record of the company's activities from the last Lexington performance in November 1813 to the first recorded

[30] Ibid., pp. 308-9.
[31] *Gazette* and *Reporter,* 19 May through 13 November 1813.

Louisville season in February 1814. Unfortunately, the Frankfort newspapers during the 1813–1814 season are missing, but since Usher performed in Lexington in November and in Louisville in February, he undoubtedly visited Frankfort with many of the same plays.

Usher's first recorded engagement in Louisville was a lengthy one which opened on February 16 and closed on April 27, 1814. With the exception of the play announcements, the Louisville papers had little to say about Usher's season there. Information is scarce concerning the old Louisville theatre, which had been used unsuccessfully by amateurs as early as 1808. It had been described as a "small establishment" on the north side of Jefferson Street between Third and Fourth streets which had "sunk into nothingness." Henrico McMurtrie states that "until the summer of 1818, it was but little better than a barn; at that time, however, it underwent alterations."[32] J. Stoddard Johnston writes that "there was a theatre in Louisville as early as 1808, but it was a miserable concern hardly fit to be attended."[33] That Louisville had any type of theatre as early as 1808 is surprising, considering the lateness of the city's growth from only 600 in 1800 to nearly 3,000 in 1814,[34] the year of Usher's first recorded season there.

On Wednesday, March 23, 1814, during her husband's spring engagement in Louisville, Mrs. Noble Luke Usher died. On Monday, March 28, 1814, the *Western Courier* announced her death:

Died

On Wed. morn. last of consumption, at the house of Mr. Joseph Scott, in the vicinity of this town, Mrs. Harriet Usher, wife of Noble Luke Usher, Manager of the Louisville Theatre, in the 30th. year of her age. She has left three infant children, an affectionate husband and numerous friends to deplore her loss.

---

[32] Henrico McMurtrie, *Sketches of Louisville and Its Environs* (Louisville, Ky., 1819), p. 126.

[33] *History of Louisville*, 1: 73.

[34] W. C. Barrickman, "Early Days in Kentucky and Elsewhere," *The Oldham Era*, 1 March 1940. Hereafter cited as "Early Days in Kentucky."

"There is another and a better World"
If a virtuous life and strict attention to moral duties give
assurance of happiness hereafter—the friends of Mrs. Usher,
have in their regret for her loss a most consoling thought.—The
corpse was conducted to the theatre at two o'clock on Thursday
last and from there to the burial ground in this town, ac-
companied by a large proportion of our most respected citizens.

Mrs. Usher's death did not prevent the company from having
a regular season of production; in fact, the theatre, operating
on Wednesday nights, offered *Catherine and Petruchio* and
Fontainville Forest on the day she died. Usher's company
performed once a week on Wednesdays, except for one Saturday
offering on May 28. Presenting the usual two plays with added
entertainment for each performance, Usher gave Louisville
twenty-two plays on eleven nights. *Hamlet,* and *The Sleep-
walker* were the only two plays given second showings during
the Louisville season. Five of the twenty-two pieces were new
to the company; the others were perennial favorites, including
The Jew, The Adopted Child, Sprigs of Laurel, Revenge, and
Adelmorn. In addition to *Hamlet* and *Catherine and Petruchio,*
Usher presented *The Merchant of Venice* and *Richard III,*
making Shakespeare the most frequently performed dramatist
of the season.[35]
Many of the plays, following the trend of the times, were
adaptations of alterations of earlier British and continental
dramas. Often there were so many translations, adaptations,
and alterations that the original became obscured. For example,
The Wanderer, or Right of Hospitality, an adaptation by
Kotzebue from a French play by Alexander Duval, was translated into German and then into English for Charles Kemble's
London production. In this melodramatic, heroic story, Sys-
imons, the Wanderer, has many adventures, all climaxed by
a spectacular battle at the castle of Valdestein. William Dunlap
adapted *The Voice of Nature* from a French play *Le jugement
de Salomon,* by L. C. Caigniez, taking the title and characters

---

[35] *Western Courier,* 16 February through 27 April 1814.

from an English piece by James Boaden, who had changed Caigniez's setting from Jerusalem to Sicily. Arthur Hobson Quinn states that Dunlap's version of *The Voice of Nature* was the first play in the United States to imitate the French *mélodrame*, a drama employing dialogue and music simultaneously.[36] Another of the season's new plays that had several hands in the making was W. C. Oulton's *The Sleepwalker, or Which Is the Lady?* a farce adapted from a French translation. Pocock's *Twenty Years Ago* and O'Keeffe's *Modern Antiques, or The Merry Mourners* complete the list of new plays offered by Usher during the 1814 season in Louisville. Pocock employed the overworked child-parent, mistaken-identity plot, and O'Keeffe repeated the traditional formula of a love intrigue assisted by rustic servants.

The little information recorded in the Louisville papers about Usher's season there reveals that the productions had the usual number of interludes, pantomimes, afterpieces, dances, and recitations. In the interlude *Tars from Tripoli* Vaughan sang "Bound Prentice to a Waterman" and Usher sang "My Nancy." As a prologue to the performance of *The Wanderer* Vaughan delivered a patriotic address written by a gentleman from Frankfort. The pantomime *Hurry Scurry, or The Village Uproar* had three performances, and interludes such as *Father Outwitted* and *Yankee Chronology* were further attractions to the regular plays. The important role of Alicia in Rowe's tragedy *Jane Shore*, the opening play of the season, was acted by Mrs. Rivers from the New York stage.[37]

Noble Luke Usher's 1814 season in Louisville fulfilled Luke Usher's dream of establishing a three-city circuit in Kentucky, the first circuit in the West. That the younger Usher was unable to hold the company together after this first successful Louisville engagement is indicated by the brief disorganized spring and summer season which followed in Lexington. After the last performance in Louisville on April 27 the Lexington Theatre was open for only three nights—Saturday, May 28,

[36] *A History of the American Drama*, p. 102.
[37] *Western Courier*, 14 February 1814.

Wednesday, June 1, and Wednesday, June 8, 1814. On these three evenings the company offered *Reconciliation, The Sleep-walker, Richard III, The Purse, The Stranger,* and *Blue Devils.*[38] A part of the Kentucky Company, as it was now called, announced in the *Louisville Correspondent* on July 6, 1814, that it intended to perform for several evenings in Louisville beginning on Saturday, July 9, with Otway's *Venice Preserved* and a two-act farce by Samuel Foote, *The Mayor of Garratt, or The Hen-pick'd Husband.* That performance, however, was delayed until Monday, August 29.

Noble Luke Usher left the company sometime after his wife's death. Whether Usher was unable to assume managerial duties during the following months or whether there were other causes for the disruption of production are questions that remain unanswered. Usher may simply have wanted to try his hand again in the theatres of the East, for Odell records that he made his debut at the Antony Street Theatre in New York as Richard III on September 22, 1814, and played Othello at the same theatre two days later. Odell describes the performance as the "Expiring of the Company in Antony Street":

> The opposition flickered, then died. It brought in Mr. Usher to play *Richard III,* on September 22nd. The quality of the performance may be gauged by the fact that Entwistle (a born comedian) played King Henry; W. Robertson (a born non-entity) played Richmond . . . Mrs. Barrett played Queen Elizabeth; and Mrs. Placide played Anne. On the 24th Usher's Othello had to combat Doyle's Iago, and was assisted by the Desdemona of Mrs. Waring. Puns are inadmissible; yet who can deny that the new actor "Ushered" out the enterprise in Antony Street?[39]

During the same season Usher was in Albany, New York, where he performed a few times in the theatre managed by his former employer, John Bernard. While acting there in such classic roles as Macbeth, Usher met Samuel Drake, Bernard's stage manager, who agreed to assume the stage management of the

---

[38] *Reporter*, 28 May 1814; *Gazette*, 30 May, 6 June 1814.
[39] Odell, *Annals of the New York Stage*, 2: 437-38.

Kentucky Circuit the following year. Drake also promised Usher that he would recruit a company and start for Kentucky during the spring of 1815. Usher was on his way back to Kentucky when he was taken ill and died in a house on the ridge of the Allegheny Mountains near Chambersburg, Pennsylvania. Luke Usher, had his son's body returned to Lexington for burial. Young Usher must have written to his father about the transaction with Drake, for after the son's death Drake received confirmation of the agreement from Luke Usher in Lexington.[40] Apparently Noble Luke Usher had intended to return to Kentucky and continue as general manager of the Kentucky Circuit. Though Noble Luke Usher's era of management ended in 1814 and was followed by a year of suspended stage activity in Kentucky, Luke Usher had reorganized the circuit by the summer of 1815, before Drake's arrival in December of the same year.

No performances took place in Kentucky between August 29, 1814, and January 16, 1815, when Lexington amateurs announced a performance of *Who Wants a Guinea?* and a new musical farce by Samuel Beazley, *The Boarding House.* The amateurs charged seventy-five cents for seats in the pit; Luke Usher reserved the boxes for his own profit in return for the use of the theatre. Another amateur production on Wednesday, April 26, 1815, was a charity benefit for "benevolent" purposes, sponsored by an unnamed group. Along with two plays, *The Honeymoon* and *The Review,* the "Young Gentlemen of Lexington" sang "Giles Scroggins Ghost," "Barney Bodkin," "Judy O'Flanagan," "Life's a Bumper," and "Briskly Beat the Hollow Drum."[41]

On April 1, 1815, an announcement in the *Western Spy,* addressed to "the Lovers of Drama," revealed that William Turner's Pittsburgh Company of Comedians, on their way to Kentucky, intended to present a few performances in Cincinnati beginning on Monday evening, April 3. For some reason Luke Usher had engaged Turner to manage the Lexington Theatre,

40 *Dramatic Life,* p. 5.
41 *Gazette,* 9 January 1815; *Reporter,* 26 April 1815.

after signing an agreement with Samuel Drake naming Drake the manager of the three-city circuit. In fact, Drake was en route to Kentucky at the same time Turner assumed the management in Lexington. Turner, who had experienced one disappointment in Usher's theatre in 1811, apparently was unaware that he was to have another in 1815.

The Turners performed in Cincinnati through May 8, 1815, in *The Stranger, Love Laughs at Locksmiths, Man and Wife, Richard III, All the World's a Stage, The Heir at Law, Pizarro,* and *Macbeth.* Turner presented one new musical entertainment in two acts, *Of Age Tomorrow,* by Thomas Dibdin. In Pittsburgh Turner had recruited a large company of players: Mr. and Mrs. Milner, Mr. and Mrs. Morgan, Collins, Jefferson, Caulfield, Cargill, Lucas, Beale, Anderson, Ludlow (not Noah M. Ludlow), Mrs. Barrett, and of course Mrs. Turner.[42] Most of these actors were unknown strolling players whose names appear later in theatrical notices throughout the West and the South. A few of them, however, were well known on eastern stages.

Mrs. George Barrett, who began her career in London, was thought to have been an acting student of the renowned Charles Macklin. She began her American career in Boston as Mrs. Beverley in *The Gamester* during the 1797 season. In New York during the same year she acted at the John Street Theatre; in 1798 she joined the company at the Park Theatre, under Dunlap's management, where she acted the role of Mrs. Haller in *The Stranger,* a part she performed with "touching pathos."[43] In Turner's company Mrs. Barrett played Mrs. Haller, Queen Elizabeth in *Richard III,* Goneril in *King Lear,* Agatha in *Lovers' Vows,* and Gertrude in *Hamlet.* After her season with Turner in 1815 she returned to the Park Theatre, where she performed "old women" roles. She died in Boston in 1832. Her son, George Barrett, was one of America's outstanding comic actors in the mid-nineteenth century.

Why a performer of Mrs. Barrett's reputation would choose

---

[42] *Western Spy,* 1, 8, 15 April, 5 May 1815.
[43] Joseph N. Ireland, *Record of the New York Stage from 1750 to 1860,* 2 vols. (New York, 1866), 1: 31-32.

to join a band of strolling players in a crude western theatre is difficult to understand. She may have reached the height of her career by 1815 and decided that a new career in the West was a possibility. Ludlow, performing in Pittsburgh with Drake's company during the fall of 1815, recalls that Mrs. Barrett visited Pittsburgh on her way east from Cincinnati after performing with Turner there. He says that she found Turner's company "poor and inadequately supported" and returned to Philadelphia, where "she was known and highly esteemed."[44] Turner's company may have been a poor one, but in fact Mrs. Barrett did not leave it after the Cincinnati season; the newspaper records show that she performed with Turner in Lexington for several months after the company had left Cincinnati.[45]

Thomas Jefferson was the oldest son of the original Joe Jefferson, the grandfather of Joe Jefferson who portrayed Rip Van Winkle. Thomas Jefferson, a stroller in Turner's company in 1815, did not inherit his father's outstanding talent, according to Ludlow, for he "was yet inefficient in his performance." Along with Francis Blisset, who later joined Turner in Lexington, Jefferson had been recruited by Samuel Drake for his Kentucky troupe. After one season with Drake in Kentucky Jefferson returned to Philadelphia, where he had performed before joining Turner.[46]

Although not a prominent actor at the time of his engagement with Turner in 1815, Joshua Collins developed into an excellent actor and manager, one of the leading theatre men of the West. His first appearance on the stage took place in Boston in 1794,[47] and after making the rounds of the eastern theatres, he joined Turner in Pittsburgh. Collins is described as a "small, Wedge-faced man, with a turned up nose, face badly pock-pitted . . . body thin, legs resembling two riding rods, his body a skeleton."[48] Despite these physical drawbacks,

[44] Dramatic Life, p. 73.
[45] Gazette, 28 August 1815.
[46] Dramatic Life, pp. 86, 83.
[47] Chronology of the American Stage, p. 37.
[48] Dramatic Life, p. 20.

he played the leading roles in *Othello, The Stranger, Hamlet,* and *King Lear.* After leaving Turner, he joined Drake in 1816, and in 1819 he formed a partnership with William Jones to manage the Cincinnati Theatre. He also managed theatres in Lexington, Nashville, and St. Louis.

The only other actor of prominence in Turner's group was Thomas Caulfield, an eccentric Englishman who died on April 22, 1815, shortly after opening the Cincinnati engagement.[49] Although he was not outstanding, he was an adequate utility actor. However, he was an excellent mimic with "a pleasant mellow-toned voice that heard to great advantage in a chamber." A Londoner by birth, Caulfield had played supporting roles at Drury Lane and Haymarket before coming to America, where he appeared at the Park Theatre in 1813 and 1814. John Bernard, Caulfield's manager in Boston recalled that he was "good in everything, but in nothing great."[50]

The *Gazette* on Monday, June 12, 1815, announced that William Turner had taken Usher's Lexington Theatre and desired the support of the community. He intended to earn this support by giving the people of Lexington respectable performances with "performers of the first celebrity on the continent, in addition to those whose talents are now offered to their attention." Ridiculous as this statement may seem, it was in some measure carried out by Turner, who managed to recruit at least two foreign stars and several excellent supporting players for his company.

Determined to make a success of his second try in Lexington, Turner produced an ambitious program of forty-five plays in twenty-four evenings from June 12 through October 9, 1815. The Lexington newspapers printed a substantial amount of information about his productions. Ten of the plays were new to Kentucky audiences, and only two—*Town and Country* and *How to Die for Love*—had second showings. Shakespeare, the most popular dramatist of the season, had five different show-ings—*King Lear, Hamlet, Othello, Henry IV,* and *The Merchant*

---

[49] "The Theatre in the Lower Valley of the Ohio," p. 21.
[50] *Retrospections of America,* pp. 294-95.

of Venice—the greatest number of Shakespearean plays ever produced in the West in a single season. Turner also revived the classic eighteenth-century plays *She Stoops to Conquer* and *The Rivals* and introduced to the Lexington stage another cele-brated English eighteenth-century drama, *The London Mer-chant, or The History of George Barnwell,* by George Lillo.[51] An extremely popular play since its first production at Drury Lane in 1731, it was performed not only in England but also on the Continent, where it "influenced the development of sentimental comedy." Though seldom performed today, *George Barnwell,* with its wages-of-sin theme, offered prize roles for Mrs. Siddons and many other stars of the period. Alexander Pope was enthusiastic in his praise for it.[52]

Turner's other new plays in 1815 included the usual farces of intrigue, exemplified by Susannah Centlivre's *The Wonder, or A Woman Keeps a Secret* and Theodore Hook's *Darkness Visible.* There were also three pieces by Thomas Morton: *The School of Reform, or How to Rule a Husband; A Cure for the Heart Ache;* and *Town and Country, Which Is Best?* The four new serious plays employed the standard sentimental traits of the period, romantic or melodramatic: James Kenny's *The Blind Boy,* a play with music; Hook's adaptation from the French, *The Fortress;* Henry Brooke's historical piece about the deliverer of Sweden, *Gustavus Vasa;* and Mrs. Frances Brooke's musical play *Rosina,* adapted from the Old Testament story of Ruth.

Examples of dialogue from two of these plays, one comedy and one so-called tragedy, display the artificial style of the times. Theodore Hook summarizes his contrived plot in *Dark-ness Visible* by having one of his characters speak directly to the audience: "So here is Ned Welford, the leader of fashions and driver of bloods, set down in a dull country-town, with matrimony, like night mare, staring him full in the face— however, I must to business. First of all I must dispatch my servant with his letter to old Seemore, the father of my in-

---

51 *Gazette* and *Reporter,* 12 June through 9 October 1815.
52 Oxford *Companion,* p. 477.

tended—a death warrant to my freedom—however, 'tis my old Dad's will and must be obeyed."

Both Dunlap and Kenny wrote plays titled *The Blind Boy.* The more popular one was Kenny's, an adaptation from the French, produced at Covent Garden in 1807 with Charles Kemble in the leading role.[53] Edmund, the blind hero, with the help of a mysterious letter is revealed to be the son of Stanislaus and heir to the throne of Sarmatia. Rudolphe, the villain and pretender to the throne, is finally foiled by Edmund's acute hearing. Elvina, in love with Edmund, reveals the hero's character in the opening words: "How beautiful are these pinks! Alas! Edmund cannot see their varied tints, but he will enjoy their fragrance. In the morning, when he opens the window, in the evening, when he reposes on this seat, the sweet perfume of the fresh flowers will assure him that Elvina ceases not to think of him."

Mr. and Mrs. Francis Blisset, two players waiting to join Drake in Frankfort, made their first appearance in Kentucky with Turner's company on July 27; Mrs. Blisset performed in *The School of Reform* and *The Citizen,* and Blisset spoke the original epilogue in the first play. Blisset was one of the few excellent actors of wide reputation who visited the West during this early period. Born in Bath, England, he made his debut on the American stage in Annapolis, Maryland, in 1793. For many years he was a great favorite on the Philadelphia stage, where he made a name for himself in farces such as A *Budget of Blunders.* A superb comedian, especially in low comic roles, he drew praise for his portrayal of Dr. Smugface in A *Budget of Blunders,* Harrowby in *The Poor Gentleman,* and Darby in *The Poor Soldier.* After playing the Drake circuit for two years, he returned to the eastern theatres and then retired to England. Like Caulfield, Blisset was a melancholy eccentric; he was also "a perfect hipocondriac."[54] These traits may have influenced him to leave a profitable position in Philadelphia

---

[53] W. Davenport Adams, A *Dictionary of the Drama* . . . (Philadelphia, 1905), p. 173.

[54] *Chronology of the American Stage,* p. 25.

for that of a stroller in a western troupe. After his celebrated comic scenes with the great Joe Jefferson in Philadelphia, Blisset must have found it disappointing in Lexington to work with another Jefferson who possessed little or no talent.

William Turner had managed to organize the largest and most talented theatrical group ever witnessed by western audiences. Not only did he have a reserve of supporting actors, but he had a substantial variety of leading players, including Mrs. Turner, Mrs. Barrett, Collins, and the Blissets. Late in the season Vaughan appeared as Hotspur in the production of *Henry IV* on October 3. The July 20 *Western Courier* had described his performance on Saturday, July 22, 1815, in the Louisville theatre as "a *satirical, Moral, instructive, comic,* and *patriotic lecture . . .* written to satirize the vices, follies, fashions, manners, customs, and eccentricities of the mimic world and [in] part to perpetuate the Sons of Columbia—interspersed with *serious, comic,* and *patriotic songs."* This lecture, *The Mirror, or A Hint to All,* was written by William Dimond, with parts added by Vaughan and someone listed as H.T. Faine.

Collins played the leading roles of Shylock, the Stranger, King Lear, and Hamlet. Mrs. Turner portrayed Portia, Ophelia, Desdemona, Countess Winterson in *The Stranger,* and Emily Tempest in *The Wheel of Fortune.* Blisset performed Jackey Hawbuck in *Town and Country,* Shelty the Piper in *Highland Reel,* Tony Lumpkin in *She Stoops to Conquer,* and Dennis Brulgruddery in *John Bull.* The relative merits of Turner's actors may be observed from the following two cast notices from the *Gazette* of July 24 and July 3, 1815:

Hamlet

Hamlet	Collins
Horatio	Morgan
Laertes	Jefferson
King	Cargill
Rosencrantz	Ludlow
Guildenstern	Anderson
Bernardo	Beale
Ghost	Lucas

Queen   Mrs. Barrett
Ophelia   Mrs. Turner

Wheel of Fortune

Penruddock	Collins
Sir David Daw	Jefferson
Governor Tempest	Lucas
Woodville	Cargill
Sydenham	Morgan
Henry Woodville	Ludlow
Weazel	Anderson
Jenkins	Beale
Mrs. Woodville	Mrs. Barrett
Emily Tempest	Mrs. Turner
Dame Dunkley	Mrs. Milner

On Monday, June 26, 1815, the *Gazette* gave Turner some lengthy publicity in connection with his production of *Lovers' Vows*. The reporter wrote that *Lovers' Vows*, a very interesting drama in five acts, surpassed all precedents in having seven translations from the German but that Mrs. Inchbald's version was preferred in London, New York, and Philadelphia. According to the article, the play was particularly interesting since "it portrays a variety of incidents and blends sentiment and humor with such nice discrimination and judgement, that it cannot but afford a rich treat to the admirers of the drama."

Turner announced in the July 31 *Gazette* that he was determined to win the encouragement of his Lexington audiences and that he was thankful for the generous support given him thus far. Because of this generosity, Turner said, he intended to use the profits from *A Cure for the Heart Ache* on July 31 for an alteration to the interior of the theatre, "which will render it commodious and agreeable." He carried out his promise, for in the August 7 *Gazette*, announcing Blisset's second appearance, he said that he hoped "the alteration of the theatre will add considerably in the convenience of the audience (the boxes and pit being entirely ready for their reception)."

Turner's understanding of the importance of publicity is

shown by his efforts to inform the public with detailed backgrounds of the plays. The August 21 announcement of *Pizarro* included a complete description of every scene. Continuing his newspaper promotion with an announcement in the August 28 *Gazette* of the celebrated patriotic and historical drama *Gustavus Vasa, the Hero of the North*, he advertised that this piece would be produced on August 29 with all the appropriate scenery, costumes, and decorations. The announcement included the information that the play had opened at Drury Lane in 1804 with a flattering reception and had been revived with alterations in dialogue and music in 1811 at Covent Garden; "fifteen crowded audiences have already approved, by an unmixed applause, the splendor of the spectacle, and the talents of the author," Turner wrote. The cast of fifteen characters utilized the entire company: Collins played Gustavus Vasa; Blisset, Maecoff; Mrs. Turner, Princess Gunilda; Barrett, Santa Michelwina; Mrs. Blisset, Frederica Rubenski; and Turner's daughter, Utrica.

Not only did Turner have a variety of acting talent in his company, but he had many performers who could dance, sing, and recite as well. Mrs. Barrett recited "The Standard of Liberty, or The American Eagle"; Mrs. Turner danced a hornpipe and recited "Choice of a Wife by Cheese"; Lucas gave a dissertation on faults, including those of the husband, old bachelor, buck, widow, wife, and spinster; Cargill sang "The American Star"; Morgan sang "Hull's Victory"; young Miss Turner also danced a hornpipe; and Blisset performed lyrical epilogues and comic songs. Turner himself who was now fully occupied with management, did not perform.

Shortly after William Turner made the agreement with Luke Usher to manage the Lexington Theatre, he discovered that Usher had made a prior arrangement with Samuel Drake; in fact, Drake announced his plans of management to the *Western Courier* in Louisville as early as June 15, 1815. Turner knew about Drake's agreement with Usher before June, however, for he filed suit against Usher on April 25, 1815. This original petition is lost, but a substitute declaration filed by

Turner on April 7, 1818, claimed that Usher had leased the three theatres in Lexington, Frankfort, and Louisville to him. Usher claimed that he had rented only the Lexington Theatre to Turner, for $200 a year in addition to the profits from the bar.[55] On October 16, 1815, the *Gazette* printed Turner's claim:

> W. Turner, for the last time, gratefully acknowledges the generous support the Company has received from the Patrons of the Drama, in Lexington, and, flattered by their liberality, is induced to inform them, that in consequence of his having contracted with Mr. Usher for the Frankfort, Louisville and Lexington Theatres, he abandoned every other prospect for the express purpose of residing with his family in Kentucky. Mr. Usher having refused him possession of the Frankfort & Louisville Theatres, he has commenced an action of damages against him, and trusts that a Jury will do HIM justice, and prove by the verdict that contracts are not to be violated with IMPUNITY.

Turner was supposed to have finished his Lexington engagement on Saturday, September 30, but he delayed it twice, first to allow Vaughan to perform Hotspur in *Henry IV*, a benefit performance for Lucas, and again on October 9, when he acknowledged in the *Gazette* the liberal encouragement he had received from his audience and stated that that evening's performance "will be positively the very last night . . . by the present company, and Mrs. Turner's last appearance in Lexington." The remark concerning Mrs. Turner suggests something of her bitterness toward Usher and Turner's disappointment after an extremely successful season in Lexington.

Blisset and Jefferson remained in Lexington after Turner's closing; while waiting for Drake, they performed on November 15 some songs and farcical recitations called "A Dramatic Olio," announced in the November 13 *Gazette*. Huntington, an actor who had played at the Lexington Theatre in 1812, announced in the *Reporter* on December 20, 1815, that he would perform in the principal western towns and that his

---

[55] Beryl Meek, "A Record of the Theatre in Lexington, Kentucky, 1790–1850" (master's thesis, University of Iowa, 1930), p. 44.

first presentation would take place in Captain Postlethwait's ballroom.

We have mentioned the sporadic theatrical production in Pittsburgh and Cincinnati, the other two important western settlements. St. Louis, with a population of approximately 2,000 in 1815, had its first amateur performance, *The School for Authors* and *A Budget of Blunders*, in January 1815 in the courthouse. Professional actors did not arrive in that city until 1818.[56] Thus in 1815 Kentucky, with the first theatre circuit in the West, continued to be the center of western stage activity.

[56] *The Theatre on the Frontier*, p. 15.

* 6 *

Arrival of the Drakes

AMERICAN stage historians usually give Samuel Drake credit for developing theatrical production in the early West. General sources such as the *Dictionary of American Biography* say that Drake was the first to bring a company of truly talented players beyond Pittsburgh.[1] An American theatrical history written as late as 1959 states that "the professional theatre in the West really began with the arrival in Frankfort in December, 1815, of Samuel Drake and his company."[2] The preceding chapters of this study have demonstrated that, on the contrary, professional as well as amateur stage companies operated in Kentucky as early as 1810 and that later ones under the managements of Douglas, Usher, and Turner sponsored successful seasons with competent companies before Drake arrived.

Many writers of early western stage history begin with Noah Miller Ludlow's account of his experiences with Drake in Kentucky in 1815 and Ludlow's subsequent management of theatres throughout the West and the South. Ludlow, an actor apprenticed to Drake, was certainly one of the first to record the story of western stage production after 1815; and inaccurate as he was at times, his information about certain stage events of the period is all that exists. It is no wonder that his valuable document has become the gospel of early western stage history. Drake never claimed to be the first professional manager in the West or to have the first organized western troupe; it was Ludlow who was fond of claiming, in almost every community he visited, that Drake's company or, later, Ludlow's was the first to organize professional drama there. Often this was true, but not always. However, these statements are not intended to deprecate the accomplishments of Samuel Drake in Kentucky and other western areas.

Information concerning Drake's birth and early life in England is scant. George D. Ford's *These Were Actors*, a fictionalized account of the Chapmans and the Drakes, says that Samuel Drake was born Samuel Bryant and that he later took the name Drake, his mother's maiden name.[3] Ford probably took his information from Ludlow, who said that Samuel Drake was born Samuel Drake Bryant in England on November 15, 1768, and that he later dropped the name Bryant.[4] John Bernard, Drake's manager in Boston and Albany, relates that Drake was born in London in 1772 and that he appeared with his wife at the Federal Street Theatre in Boston during the 1810-1811 season.[5] Ford's romantic treatment of the Chapmans and the Drakes asserts that Drake was born in Barnstaple, England, and studied theology at Oxford University. George Colman, a friend of young Drake, took him to Covent Garden, Ford continues, where he saw his first play, Shakespeare's *Hamlet*. He fell in love with Miss Alexina Fisher, who was playing Ophelia, gave up theology, began his stage career at Bath, and married Miss Fisher.[6] However, had Drake studied at Oxford or had he been on intimate terms with the renowned George Colman, Ludlow surely would have known it and mentioned it in his account. Ludlow simply relates that Drake was apprenticed as a printer (like many aspiring actors of the period), ran away from his apprenticeship, joined an acting troupe, became a manager of a provincial company in the west of England, and married Miss Fisher, whose brother was a theatre manager in Exeter, England.[7] This information is all

---

[1] DAB, 5: 432.
[2] Barnard Hewitt, *Theatre, U.S.A.: 1668 to 1957* (New York, 1959), p. 88.
[3] George D. Ford, *These Were Actors* (New York, 1955), p. xx.
[4] *Dramatic Life*, p. 363.
[5] *Retrospections of America*, p. 364.
[6] Ford, *These Were Actors*, pp. 167-68, 93-95.
[7] *Dramatic Life*, p. 363.

that is actually known about Drake before his arrival in America in 1810.

During the 1810-1811 season at the Federal Street Theatre in Boston Drake's name appears along with "other new importations . . . Mrs. Doidge [also spelled Doige, who performed in Lexington in 1812], and others of more or less ability."[8] There on January 3, 1811, Mrs. Drake (Alexina Fisher) played the Duchess of York to George Frederick Cooke's Richard III; her son Alexander made his debut as Prince Edward in the same play.[9] Drake remained in Boston under the management of Dickenson, Powell, and Bernard until 1813, when Bernard became manager of the Albany Theatre in New York. Drake moved to Albany with Bernard and served as his stage manager there. Little is recorded of Drake's acting roles or of his other production responsibilities in Albany; however, it is known that in addition to his stage managing he performed the roles of King Lear and Julius Caesar.[10]

In 1814 all was not going well for Drake in Albany. Mrs. Drake died that year, Bernard was ready for retirement, and Drake's position with the Albany Theatre seemed none too certain. Thus when Noble Luke Usher visited Albany in the fall of 1814 and offered Drake a position in a western venture, he agreed to organize a company, make the trip to Kentucky the following spring, and "enter upon the duties of stage-manager in the employ of Mr. Usher."[11] But Noble Luke Usher died on his way back to Kentucky, and his father hired Drake as the general manager of the circuit. At this time Drake was forty-five years of age. Although he had just reached middle age and was to live to eighty-six, he was spoken of by Ludlow and others in the early years as "Old Drake," a title which may have been given him to avoid confusion with Samuel Drake, Jr., his oldest son.

In order to arrive in Frankfort during the meeting of the

8 *Retrospections of America*, p. 354.
9 William W. Clapp, Jr., *A Record of the Boston Stage* (Boston, 1853), p. 123.
10 Henry Pitts Phelps, *Players of a Century: A Record of the Albany Stage* (Albany, N.Y., 1880), pp. 48-50. Hereafter cited as *Players of a Century*.
11 *Dramatic Life*, p. 5.

State Legislature in December 1815, Drake left Albany in May 1815, allowing himself time for performances along the way. Finding it difficult to recruit actors for such an insecure venture, he had to rely mainly on the support of his five children, who ranged in age from about thirteen to twenty-one. In addition to his family, Drake hired Mr. and Mrs. Lewis, Miss Frances Ann Denny, Joe Tracy, and Noah M. Ludlow. Lewis acted as general manager, Tracy served as stage carpenter, Mrs. Lewis played elderly roles, Miss Denny acted juvenile parts, and Ludlow doubled as advance agent and utility actor.[12] The Drake children, aside from acting roles (sometimes, but not always, suiting their own ages), sang, danced, and played musical instruments. Drake had arranged for other actors— Blisset, Jefferson, and the Vaughans—to meet him in Frankfort.

Transportation in 1815 was difficult enough between cities in the East, but a theatrical troupe traveling from Albany, New York, to Frankfort, Kentucky, carrying scenery, properties, equipment, and personal belongings over mountains and down rivers into a newly settled wilderness, was a trek "that was probably the most heroic in the annals of the American Stage."[13] Traveling northwest from Albany by stagecoach, Drake covered forty miles the first day and spent the night at Cherry Valley, New York. Here Ludlow erected the three-foot platform in front of the judge's desk in the courthouse. He unrolled the six different scenes painted on backdrops and matched them with folding wings, all set within a portable proscenium opening which was adjustable to fit any theatre, ballroom, or courthouse. The floor of the acting area was covered with a green baize carpet. All could be packed away within two hours.[14] On the first evening at Cherry Valley Drake offered *The Prize, or 2,5,3,8* and *The Purse;* the second night gave eighteen-year-old Frances Ann Denny the opportunity to play the leading role of Julia in *The Midnight Hour.* Along with Ludlow, she was the only novice in the company. Little did anyone realize

[12] Ibid., p. 8.
[13] DAB, p. 432.
[14] Dramatic Life, pp. 7-8.

that she would become an actress of such nationwide reputation that she would be called "the Siddons of the West."

At Cooperstown, New York, the company repeated *The
Prize,* and Ludlow had to take a part usually played by Sam
Drake, Jr. This was his first attempt at acting, and his mind
went blank after his first entrance. Samuel Drake, seeing the
young man's difficulty, carried off the scene as only a stock
actor of the period could do: "Mr. Drake, seeing my situation,—
that I was, in stage parlance, 'struck dead,'—said: 'pray, Captain,
don't speak; I know you are too unwell to exert yourself, that is
why I am called in; I understand what you would say;' and
then he would repeat enough of my speech to enable himself
to reply to it . . . the audience . . . never knew but that it was
not all so intended."[15] This frightened actor, who recorded the
more adventuresome scenes of western theatre in *Dramatic Life
As I Found It,* notes that James Fenimore Cooper sat in the
audience at the Cooperstown performance.[16]

Making their way by wagon, the actors moved westward
across New York, performing in Herkimer, Utica, Onondago
Hollow (apparently there is no longer a town of this name),
Manlius, Skaneateles, Auburn, Geneva, and Canandaigua. According to Ludlow, they were the first to introduce the drama
into this area.[17] At Skaneateles Drake performed in the ballroom, and at Canandaigua they were back in the county courthouse, where Miss Denny played the title role in Monk Lewis's
Adelgitha, her first tragic part. Ludlow, in his praise for Miss
Denny, remarks that she performed this role better than anyone he had ever seen.[18]

At Olean, New York, Drake traded his wagon for a flat-
bottomed boat, and in July the troupe headed down the Allegheny River to Pittsburgh, some 200 miles downstream. When
they finally reached Pittsburgh, after some frightening experiences with wolves, waterfalls, and irate farmers, they dis-

---

[15] Ibid., p. 10.
[16] Ibid., p. 9.
[17] Ibid., p. 10.
[18] Ibid., p. 12.

covered that the city was not the restful haven they had expected:

> It is well known to everyone who visited Pittsburgh, even in
> its later and improved days, that, owing to the quantity of
> coals consumed in and about the city, there is scarcely a build-
> ing but presents a somber or almost black appearance. At the
> period of our arrival it was badly lighted at night, and where
> there was a light it served only to show what then appeared
> to us the "horrors of the place." Every house, inside as well as
> out, appeared begrimed with soot. Even the faces we saw had
> a shade of darkness, that gave them an appearance of anything
> rather than pleasant. All was hot and dirty.[19]

The Pittsburgh theatre that had been occupied by Turner
and amateurs offered no more hope than did the town. It was
located on the outskirts of the city, facing Fifth Street, not
far from Wood Street. A pit and one tier of boxes comprised
the interior of the building, and "the form was after the old
style,—two parallel elongations, with an elliptical curve at the
entrance."[20] At the time Turner had performed in this theatre
in 1812 it had been advertised as a "New Theatre," but three
years later Ludlow described the decorations as being of "the
plainest kind, and every portion bore the Pittsburg stamp upon
it."[21] (Though Turner had performed sporadically in Pittsburgh beginning in 1812, he apparently was happy to return
to Lexington in 1815.) Repeating his frequently stated claim,
Ludlow asserts that Drake's season in Pittsburgh, beginning in
mid-August 1815, "was the first attempt at any regular, pro-
tracted season that had been made in that city. There had
been some performances for a limited number of nights by
different strollers, assisted by such amateurs as were there to
be found, anxious to display their extraordinary abilities. It
could not be said that the Drama commenced its reign there
till the season of Mr. Drake's."[22]

[19] Ibid., p. 51.
[20] Ibid., p. 55.
[21] Ibid.
[22] Ibid., p. 61.

Five strollers joined the company in time to assist with the opening: Mrs. Mary Riddle, Mr. and Mrs. Williams, and two unnamed, inexperienced players. Williams may have been the same actor who had performed with Douglas in Lexington in 1810. Mrs. Riddle, a Philadelphian, was the mother of Eliza Riddle, who later became a popular actress in St. Louis and Mobile.[23]

Operating in Pittsburgh with an inadequate company, Drake managed to produce such favorites as *The Honeymoon; The Castle Spectre; Pizarro; Speed the Plough; No Song, No Supper;* and others.

Williams was determined to play Rolla in *Pizarro* despite Drake's apprehension concerning the difficulties of producing the elaborate piece. In addition to the scenic problems demanded by the temple of the sun, the cast called for several extras to play the temple virgins. Old Drake finally consented to do the play. He painted the scenery and cast the play, with the exception of the virgins, a chore left to Williams. In the performance all went well until the entrance of the virgins, heralded by slow, dramatic music. Williams had recruited Mrs. Lewis, an elderly lady; Miss Denny; Miss Julia Drake, age fourteen; Martha Drake, whom Ludlow says was thirty, but who must have been much younger; and two extras, the property man and an Irish woman who cleaned the dressing rooms. The virgins were costumed in long white cotton gowns, red sashes, large golden suns affixed to their breasts, and gauze veils. Silence reigned during the ritual until the cleaning woman and the property man made their entrance. "There was heard to arise from the centre of the pit a long and pious groan, and a voice, partially subdued, but loud enough to be heard in the prevailing silence, 'Oh, such virgins!' The effect was not unlike that of dropping a lighted match into a canister of gunpowder,— the explosion was tremendous. The pit shouted and the house roared with laughter, in which the actors were compelled to join."[24]

[23] Ibid., p. 272.
[24] Ibid., p. 67.

In a performance of *The Quaker* Samuel Drake, Jr., was forced to play violin music offstage while speaking the lines of Lubin. He accomplished this feat by playing the violin just out of sight and thrusting his head in from the wings to speak.[25] Bad as these Pittsburgh productions must have been, Drake's players prepared a repertory of plays for the Kentucky Circuit, surviving the inconvenience of doubling in roles and the embarrassment of employing charwomen as extras.

The exact dates of Drake's Pittsburgh engagement are not known, but he arrived there in August 1815 and left for Kentucky in mid-November. Drake acquired another boat, and after floating down the Ohio River for a week, he landed his company at Limestone, Kentucky (now Maysville), where he traded the boat for a wagon. The friendly Kentuckians drew glowing praise from Ludlow, who performed in the state for the next two seasons and later visited it frequently:

> I have never found a more kind and hospitable people than those in Kentucky, generally, and I have travelled in most all States of the Union. It seemed to me in after years, when I had visited most of the Western, Southern, and Northern States, that Kentucky, as a State, could boast of more high-minded men and beautiful women than any I had ever been in. I have found there more genuine and unostentatious hospitality than in any other State, and that dispensed by princely men and courtly women, stamped with nobility by the hand of their Creator.[26]

Drake and his troupe arrived in Frankfort during the latter part of November, and on Monday, December 4, 1815, he announced the opening of the Frankfort Theatre:

THEATRE

Mr. Drake, late Director of the Theatres at Boston & Albany respect. informs ladies & gents of the State of Ky that he intends to estab. the drama on a permanent & regular plan & for this purpose has brought with him a company of well known talent

25 Ibid., p. 63.
26 Ibid., p. 78.

& unblemished reputation. The selection of his pieces will be duly attended to & a decided preference given to those where moral tendency is inculcated & where instruction is blended with innocent amusement.

Frankfort Theatre

Mon eve Dec 4, 1815[27]

The company began the season the same day with *The Mountaineers, or Love and Madness* by Colman and *The Midnight Hour, or Ruse Contra Ruse* by Mrs. Inchbald. The December 4 *Palladium* noted that *The Mountaineers* was "interspersed with music." The *Palladium* printed only two other theatrical notices that season—one on Monday, December 11, announcing *Speed the Plough* and *Of Age Tomorrow;* and one on Monday, December 18, announcing *The Merchant of Venice* and *The Purse, or The American Tar.*[28] Ludlow is correct about the opening play, *The Mountaineers,* but his memory failed him concerning the second play, which he listed as O'Keeffe's *The Poor Soldier.* The only other play mentioned by Ludlow which did not appear in the three newspaper announcements was Colman's *Ways and Means.* Though the Frankfort newspapers failed to list any cast, Ludlow recorded the complete cast of *The Mountaineers:*

Octavian	John Vaughan
Bulcazan Muley	Mr. S. Drake
Count Virolet	Mr. Jefferson
Rocque	Mr. Drake
Kilmallock	Mr. Ludlow
Lope Toche	Mr. Blissett
Sadi	Aleck Drake
Lady Zorayda	Miss Martha Drake
Floranthe	Miss Denny
Agnes	Mrs. Lewis
Muleteers and	H. Vaughan and James
Messengers	Drake, and others[29]

[27] John J. Weisert, "Beginnings of the Kentucky Circuit," *Filson Club History Quarterly* 34 (July 1960): 280.
[28] *Palladium,* 11, 18 December 1815 (John J. Weisert's unpublished notes from Frankfort newspapers).
[29] *Dramatic Life,* pp. 83, 81-82.

James Douglas, Thomas Jefferson, Francis Blisset, John Vaughan, and Vaughan's younger brother Henry joined Drake during the Frankfort engagement. The Vaughans and Ludlow left Drake's company to barnstorm the South after the second season in Kentucky. Douglas continued to perform with Drake for several seasons until 1820, when he drowned in the Wabash River at Vincennes, Indiana, where the company was engaged for the summer. At the time of his death Douglas was earning six dollars a week as a supporting actor.[30] Jefferson returned to Philadelphia at the end of Drake's first engagement in Frankfort.[31]

Ludlow is incorrect with his date of March 1, 1816, for the closing of the Frankfort Theatre, for Drake began his Louisville engagement on Wednesday, February 28, 1816, according to the *Western Courier* of the same date. Drake had prepared the Louisville citizens for his arrival as early as June 15, 1815, with an announcement in the *Courier*:

CARD

The Ladies and Gentlemen of Louisville and its vicinity, the proprietors of the theatre and the public in general, are respectfully informed that I have purchased the time which Mr. Usher had in the Kentucky theatres, and that I commenced a journey of a thousand miles, for the express purpose of establishing theatrical amusements on a respectable and permanent plan—where the eye shall revel in fancys fairy bower, and the heart expand in scenes of luxurious delight. No expense of dresses, scenery, or decorations, shall ever be neglected, that will in the least contribute to the entertainment of the public. I trust my assiduous endeavors, joined by my itinerant friends, Vaughan, Douglas, and a company which I flatter myself by proving of the first standing, will receive that patronage which is the characteristic of a generous public. Relying on a universal approbation, the proprietors and Trustees, will, I hope, so far befriend our absent wanderer, to prevent invaders from any attack on those theatres, which I now consider as mine,

30 *Theatrical Management*, p. 39.
31 *Dramatic Life*, p. 83.

and which I shall open at a proper season. The joint efforts of all persons, will, (I do not hesitate to say) eradicate those impressions which have hitherto reigned too predominant, and fix an eulogium on the Theatres, little inferior to those in eastern states.

With most profound respect,
I remain, the Proprietors,
Trustees, and the Public's
Most Humble and
Devoted servant,
S. Drake
Albany (N.Y.) April 27th, 1815

According to Ludlow, there was no stagecoach from Frankfort to Louisville in 1815, and the company, traveling by horseback and wagon, made the fifty-mile trip in two days. The citizens of Louisville were anxious for the theatre to open, but their theatre, like those in Pittsburgh and Frankfort, had been closed for a long time and was not ready for use. Ludlow's alliterative description called it "dark, dingy, and dirty." In fact, it was such a poor place that Drake refurbished it completely in 1818. Not only was the scenery in bad condition, but the auditorium was poorly lighted and needed paint.[32] Drake ran into John Vos, the actor, manager, and house painter who had advertised his coach and house painting business in the *Courier* as early as January 12, 1815, having abandoned the theatre for the paint trade in Lexington after the 1812 season. Drake hired him to renovate the Louisville theatre and to serve as a supporting actor. Vos returned to the stage with Drake's company in Louisville during the 1816 season, receiving favorable notices from the critics. He went to St. Louis as a house painter in 1818 and there joined Turner for another stint of acting. After making the rounds of various southern and western theatres with his wife and daughter, both performers, Vos died in 1826.[33]

Drake's second Louisville announcement, in the *Western*

[32] Ibid., p. 88.
[33] Ibid., p. 287.

Citizen on February 7, 1816, leaves no doubt about his intention to control the Kentucky Circuit:

THEATRICAL

The very respectable company of Comedians, now in Frankfort, are about to open our theatre—general reports are loud in their praise.—Mr. Drake, the manager, has, we understand, made a purchase of Mr. Usher's right of the whole of the Kentucky theatres,—He has brought his company for the express purpose of establishing the business upon a firm and permanent plan; and we seriously congratulate the lovers of the drama upon the prospect of a well governed rational amusement. We have no hesitation to assert an opinion, that the same happy welcome which this company has merited & received in Frankfort, will be extended to them in Louisville.

While Drake was performing in Frankfort, Luke Usher advertised in the January 15, 1816, *Gazette* that his Lexington Theatre, along with his house adjoining it, would be sold at auction. The *Gazette* described the property as consisting of the theatre, the house, part of a peach orchard, and a number of bonds. Though Usher stated in the advertisement that everything "will be positively be [*sic*] sold *without reserve*," he failed to sell the theatre. As late as May 29, 1819, he advertised in the *Gazette* that the Lexington Theatre was for lease "to any genteel company who may apply first." Thus Usher obviously intended to relinquish his theatrical interests. Although Drake had acquired control of the Frankfort and Louisville theatres, he failed to get control of Usher's Lexington Theatre. Perhaps this was one reason he chose Louisville for his home and his base for theatrical operations in Kentucky and other areas. Of course, Louisville, with approximately 3,000 people in 1816,[34] was rapidly becoming the principal western center of industry and transportation, a fact which may also have influenced Drake.

Again on Wednesday, February 21, 1816, Drake informed the *Western Courier* that he intended to open the Louisville

[34] "Early Days in Kentucky."

Theatre on the following Monday, but there was a delay until Wednesday, February 28, at which time he began his first Louisville season with *The Heir at Law* and *The Midnight Hour*. In the February 28 *Courier* Drake referred to himself as "late director of Boston and Albany," a statement which stretched the truth considerably. After stating again that he would establish the drama upon a regular and permanent plan, Drake announced that he intended to tour the important Kentucky towns each year with his group of professionals and that he had chosen a selection of plays with a "decided preference given to those where sentiment of a moral tendency is emulated, and where instruction is blended with innocent amusement."

During his first Louisville engagement Drake produced twenty-four plays in twelve evenings beginning on February 28 and ending on May 14, 1816. Of the twenty-four pieces, only five were new to Kentucky audiences: *Robin Hood and Little John*, *The Lying Valet*, *The Quaker*, *The Kiss*, and *Adrian and Orilla*. The company revived the popular *Blind Boy*, *The Midnight Hour*, *Reconciliation*, *The Castle Spectre*, *The Poor Gentleman*, and others. *The Midnight Hour* and *The Blind Boy* were the only plays given second showings.

We have noted that some popular plays had many versions, all by different authors. Frequently the newspapers failed to mention the name of the playwright. Often managers added second titles and improvised descriptions of the pieces. A good example is the anonymous musical play announced by Drake in the March 6 *Courier* as *Robin Hood and Little John, or The Merry Foresters of Sherwood Forest*, with "original music, vocal and instrumental." Allardyce Nicoll's *History of the English Drama* lists twenty different plays with the title *Robin Hood*. One is titled *Robin Hood and Little John*, but none has the second title, probably improvised, announced by Drake.[35] Solomon Smith, one of Drake's rival managers in the early

[35] Allardyce Nicoll, *A History of the English Drama, 1660–1900* (Cambridge, 1959), vol. 6, *A Short-Title Alphabetical Catalogue of Plays Produced or Printed in England from 1660 to 1900*, pp. 431-32.

West, recalls that Drake was fond of adding his own second titles to plays. To Tobin's *The Honeymoon* he added *The Painter and His Three Daughters*; to *The Hunters of the Alps* he added *The Runaway Horse That Flung Its Rider in the Forest of Savoy*; and to the title of Shakespeare's *Richard III* he once contributed a second title which described almost the entire play.[36]

The other new plays followed the sentimental and farcical tradition of the period. *The Lying Valet* by Garrick and *The Kiss, or Beware of Jealousy* by Stephen Clarke are both farcical pieces employing complicated situations. Garrick's afterpiece involves a servant and his master in a fortune-seeking intrigue, and Clarke's five-act comedy borrows a plot of Spanish intrigue and mistaken identity from Fletcher and Massinger. Charles Dibdin's comic opera *The Quaker* employs the overworked story of a love match that is opposed by the girl's parents, who want her to marry a rich Quaker; all is resolved when the Quaker decides the case in favor of the young lovers. *Adrian and Orilla* is a sentimental tale by William Dimond dealing with a woman and her lost child, a theme he used again in *The Foundling of the Forest*. The company added the usual songs and other entertainment to the regular plays. James Drake sang "Kitty of Clyde," "Tell Her I Love Her," and "Loves of Sandy and Gliney." Frances Ann Denny delivered a comic recitation called "An Occasional Address."[37]

On March 6, after the opening in Louisville, the *Courier* critic commented on the crowded audience, the improvements in scenery and decorations, the "judicious" management of Drake, and the "display of acknowledged talents possessed by the present company." On March 13 the *Courier* praised Mrs. Lewis and Blisset for their portrayals of Madame Clermont and Dr. Pangloss in *The Heir at Law*: Blisset's ability to play the pompous, pedantic mock doctor was admirably displayed, and Mrs. Lewis "possessed no ordinary share of professional talents"

[36] *Theatrical Management*, p. 28.
[37] *Western Courier*, 20 March, 5 April 1816. Hereafter cited as *Courier*. *Louisville Correspondent*, 11 March 1816.

in her show of sympathetic tears. She used the appropriate voice, movement, gesticulation, and countenance. Samuel Drake, Sr., did "justice" to all his parts and possessed all the requisites of a "chastened performance"; his roles of Sheva in *The Jew* and Bertram in *The Foundling of the Forest* "equalled the best in the country." Alexander Drake was complimented for his broad humor as the servant in *The Lying Valet*; the critic went so far as to rank him with the great Joe Jefferson as a low comedian. Vaughan, the company's leading man, appeared to have some misconceptions of his roles and projected some of them in an affected manner. His bombastic and pompous playing of Guiscard in *Adelgitha*, however, was judged good. Ludlow was considered good in genteel comedy; Jefferson had less grace and animation than was expected from a performer of his experience, but his acting of Bertram was admired. As Miss Bertram, Miss Denny was considered animated and interesting, but she was warned to give closer attention to the dialogue. Other brief remarks by the *Courier* critic reveal that Douglas was best in delineating old men and that Julia Drake had a sweet voice and correct judgment of roles. Samuel Drake, Jr., was handsome on the stage but too young to be convincing; time, however, would improve him.[38]

One other item of importance in connection with this first Louisville season is an article in the April 10 *Courier* debating the merits of a city tax levied against Drake. The writer was opposed to it on the grounds that it had been imposed before the time of the regular circuit as a protection to the city from imposters, charlatans, vagabonds, and "corrupters of the morals of the Community." He believed that Drake's company had a "beneficial effect on the town" and that the tax should be removed. Later Drake originated charity benefit performances as a means of escaping this tax in all three cities.

After the final performance of *The Merchant of Venice* in Louisville on May 14, 1816, the Drake company lost no time in moving to Lexington for a summer season. Before the engagement in Louisville was over, an article appeared in the

[38] *Courier*, 27 March, 25 April 1816.

Gazette on April 29 announcing the forthcoming Lexington visit by the Drakes:

> With pleasure we announce, that the Theatrical Corps, under the direction of Mr. DRAKE (late Manager of the Boston and Albany Theatres) will commence their campaign in this place in about three weeks. From the acknowledged taste and judgment of the Manager and the well earned performers, the Ladies and Gentlemen of Lexington and its vicinity, may safely promise themselves a source of real delight. If any thing could add to our gratification, it is the hope that our friend COLLINS (who is now a resident of our neighborhood) will engage during Mr. Drake's stay in this place—and from the high opinion we have formed of the latter gentleman, we have no doubt, he will avail himself of the opportunity to obtain so valuable an acquisition.

That Drake was making good use of his advance agent, Ludlow, is obvious from such preseason notices in all three Kentucky towns. Collins, who had been acting with the Turner group in Cincinnati, did join Drake in Lexington in 1816.

The company traveled again by horseback and wagon from Louisville to Lexington to open the theatre there on May 21, 1816. Ludlow describes their first meeting with Luke Usher— brewer, innkeeper, umbrella maker, and theatrical producer:

> Mr. Luke Usher met us with great cordiality, and welcomed us to the metropolis of Kentucky with a considerable flourish of trumpets; whether there were any cannons fired, I cannot now recollect. But certainly we were persons of distinction in the estimation of Mr. Usher, who introduced us all, and to every body, without regard to age, rank, nation, tongue, or color. With the exception of his knocking about the h's rather strangely, having been born within sound of "Bow bells,"—he was somewhat a country gentleman—a "fine old English gentleman, one of the olden time." He was a man of large hospitality, and a heart in proportion to his body, which later was of the Falstaffian model; and his wife was no less remarkable for size and generosity. I remember with a good deal of pleasure the delicious plum-pudding I ate at her table, when she used

to sit and deal out the smoking, fragrant dish with a liberal hand, and with broad, smiling good-natured face, that plainly said to you in her homely way, "you're heartily welcome."[39]

If the friendly meeting with Luke Usher lifted the spirits of the homesick troupe, their first visit to the "brewery" theatre must have had the opposite effect, judging from Ludlow's unflattering description (see chapter three). Nevertheless, Drake must have felt somewhat relieved to see that the Lexington Theatre was at least in better condition than the ones in Louisville and Pittsburgh.

After the usual renovation of the theatre and an announcement to the newspapers (almost the same as the one he had used in Louisville and Frankfort), Drake advertised in the May 20 *Gazette* the opening of the Lexington Theatre on Monday, May 21, 1816, with *The Foundling of the Forest* and *The Poor Soldier*. The summer heat forced an early closing of the engagement on July 1, but Drake remained in Lexington for a second season beginning in September before the opening of the Frankfort Theatre in December. All the plays presented by Drake during his first season in Lexington had been seen by Kentucky audiences in past seasons, and only *Man and Wife* and *The Kiss* were new to the Lexington Theatre. Between some of the plays, reported the June 24 *Gazette*, Master James Drake sang his regular songs and added a new one called "Tom Starboard," and his older brother Alexander sang a comic song, "What Is, and What Is Not the Dandy O." The Lexington newspapers praised Drake for his industry and perseverance in developing an excellent company. No reviews came from the newspapers, but the notice in the May 27 *Gazette* mentioned that two of the first three performances had crowded houses; "the selections were judicious; and the performance upon each occasion, met with truly gratifying response."

Drake must have produced more plays during the spring and summer season in Lexington than the newspapers announced, for on May 27, 1816, the *Gazette* announced that the theatre

[39] *Dramatic Life*, p. 90.

had been open for three nights; only one notice had appeared (on Monday), but two performances had taken place (on Tuesday and Wednesday). *Othello*, announced for Wednesday, June 5, by the *Reporter*, failed to be mentioned by the *Gazette*. On June 3 Drake announced in the *Gazette* that for the remaining period of the company's engagement the theatre would be open on Monday, Wednesday, and Saturday; but no Saturday notices appeared in the Lexington newspapers.

While waiting for the opening of the second engagement in Lexington, Ludlow, anxious for more experience, borrowed some scenery and a few actors from Drake and went on a barnstorming tour of the bluegrass area. At Danville the troupe opened with *The Midnight Hour* and *The Poor Soldier*. Ludlow describes Danville as having about 1,000 people in 1816, "all in comfortable circumstances."[40] Moving to Paris, Kentucky, after performing three times a week for sixteen days in Danville, at Davenport's Hotel or the courthouse, Ludlow occupied the Paris Hotel ballroom for a performance of *The Gamester* and some unnamed pieces.[41] He and the actors were back in Lexington in September, ready for the fall season.

The second season opened on September 30 with *Adrian and Orilla* and *The Liar*. In the September 23 *Gazette* Drake made the usual promises to "the lovers of drama" that he would give them a variety of new and interesting pieces with "elegant dresses, scenery, and decorations." The engagement played through November 26, with performances mainly on Tuesdays; three productions took place on Mondays, one on a Thursday, and one on a Wednesday. A benefit performance for Vaughan introduced a new musical farce "never performed in the Country," *Lock and Key, or Nothing Venture–Nothing Have* by Prince Hoare, with music by William Shield. Four other new plays added variety to Drake's repertory: *The Liar*, a two-act farce by Samuel Foote; *The Agreeable Surprise, or The Learned Butler*, another of O'Keeffe's comic operas; *The Miller and His*

40 Ibid., p. 96.
41 Ibid., p. 98.

Men, or The Bohemian Robber, a romantic melodrama by Isaac Pocock; and a farce by Charles Kemble called *Plot Counterplot, or The Portrait of Cervantes.*[42] Drake repeated *Macbeth, Hamlet, The Busy Body, The Mountaineers,* and other favorites.

In the *Macbeth* notice, appearing in the October 7 *Gazette,* Drake revealed that the production would use a chorus and instrumental music to perform the original songs in the play. Since Shakespeare's *Macbeth* has no original songs Drake may have been referring to the music in some later alteration of the play, such as Davenant's seventeenth-century operatic version. Drake and his family made the most of their musical talents during the engagement in Lexington. Alexander Drake sang his favorite, "Bag of Nails," along with "Call Again Tomorrow." Blisset presented "What a Woman Is Like" and "Thomas Chutterbuck and Polly Higenbottom." In act two of *The Castle Spectre* everyone joined in a glee entitled "Megen Oh! Megen Eh!" and at the end of the piece Ludlow and Alexander performed a musical dialogue "Gaffer Grey." At the conclusion of *The Busy Body,* according to the November 18 *Gazette,* several of the players sang a song announced as "The Catch Club, or Mirth and Harmony":

Catch—"Fill everyman," by Messrs S. Drake and Blisset
Comic Round—"Old Thomas Day," by Alexander, Blissett, Ludlow
Catch—"Oh, how Sophia (alias) a house on fire," Blissett, S. Drake, and Bridge
Glee—"Oh, why to be happy," by the company
Comic Round—"Here's a Health to all good Lassies"

Other newspapers revealed that Ludlow spoke a "Dissertation on Faults"; in *Man and Wife* Collins played the leading role, Sir Willoughby Worret, and Mrs. Lewis acted Lady Worret; on the same evening Collins played Petruchio in *Catherine and Petruchio,* and Frances Denny performed Cath-

[42] *Reporter,* 13 November 1816.

erine. Collins also took the lead as Octavian in *The Mountaineers*, supported by Mrs. Vaughan as Lady Zorayda.[43] Illness prevented Julia Drake from performing much during the Lexington season. A notice in the November 25 *Gazette* said that she had undergone "a long and continued illness" but that she should not be forgotten:"She is a bud of sweet promise, and if nurtured by the hand of philanthropy, will one day expand into the full bloom of ornament and delight."

There are only two other theatrical notices concerning Drake's performers during the fall engagement in Lexington. One, in the November 13 *Gazette*, announced Alexander Drake's benefit performance of Lewis's *The Castle Spectre* on November 14:

> Lexington now has opportunity of shewing that an unimpeachable reputation in a young man, united with anxious disposition to please the public, shall never go unrewarded. We trust it will be remembered that Mr. Alexander is a young man scrupulously correct in his moral character, combining in his profession an almost universality, with superiority of talent which enables him to feel strongly and act naturally any character for which he may be cast. But were his merit in other respects much less than it is, his ambition combined with application, which make him familiar with his parts to that degree, that on the stage he is enabled to make just approbation and proper discrimination entitle him to high regard and esteem, and when it is considered how much in this particular he excells almost all his fellow actors, we trust he will not go unrewarded.
>
> *Stage Box*

Drake used the full company and two extras in this production, for which a cast list appeared in the November 13 *Reporter*:

Earl Osmond	Mr. S. Drake, Jr.
Earl Reginald	Collins
Earl Percy	Ludlow
Father Philip	Sam Drake, Sr.
Motley	Alexander Drake

[43] *Gazette*, 21 October, 11 November 1816; *Reporter*, 20 November 1816.

Kenric	Douglas
Muley	Blisset
Hassan	Vaughan
Saib	H. Vaughan
Alaric	Francis
Angela	Miss Denny
Alice	Mrs. Lewis
Elvina	Miss Clark

Performing between 75 and 100 plays (the number in Frankfort is unknown) during his first season in Kentucky, Drake maintained the state's position as the theatrical center of the early West. In fact, during the extremely successful engagements of the Turners and the Drakes in 1815 and 1816, little drama production occurred in other established western towns. New Orleans, a much older and larger city than any in Kentucky, had "amateur performances which from 1812 to 1817 constituted the only theatrical activity in English," only nine plays and one interlude.[44] As we have noted, St. Louis had no professional drama until 1818, and the amateurs there, beginning as late as 1815, produced only eight plays within the next two years.[45] Cincinnati had no professional stage performances after the Turner engagement in 1815. On October 13, 1815, the *Western Spy* announced a pantomime, *The Black Forest*, by a performer named Perez who also exhibited grand feats of "Tight Rope." Cincinnati's amateurs produced eight plays and a pantomime in January, March, and April 1816.[46]

All appeared to be going well for Drake. He had made the complete circuit with successful engagements in Frankfort, Louisville, and Lexington. In addition to the regular schedule, he had sent his players into rural areas to perform where no professional productions had appeared before. The professional theatre in Kentucky was flourishing.

[44] Nellie Smither, *A History of the English Theatre in New Orleans* (New York, 1967), pp. 10-11.

[45] *The Theatre on the Frontier*, pp. 15-18.

[46] *Western Spy*, 29 March, 13 October 1815; "The Theatre in the Lower Valley of the Ohio," appendix.

* 7 *

Drake's Western Theatrical Empire

AMUEL DRAKE's talented family contributed much to the success of his western stage venture. His three sons, his younger daughter, and later his daughter-in-law possessed the variety of acting and musical ability required for the demanding theatrical presentations of the day. Often they were called upon to act, sing, dance, recite, and play musical instruments in one evening. The Drake children, reared as English strollers, learned their trade almost before they learned to walk. By the time they reached Kentucky they had doubled in roles, performed a variety of parts, acted new characters with little or no preparation, and performed in various places from ill equipped theatres to courthouses; they were well prepared for the challenges and rigors of the Kentucky Circuit.

Not much is known about Martha Drake, the oldest of the children. Born in England around 1795,[1] she was nearly twenty when she made the journey west with the other members of her family. Although she performed supporting roles in the various productions on the western journey, she was not a talented actress, nor was she interested in making a career of the stage. Shortly after arriving in Kentucky, she married an English merchant named Duckham who had opened a business in Frankfort. They returned to England several years after the opening of the Kentucky Circuit.[2]

Samuel Drake, Jr., the eldest son, was born in 1796. Having musical ability, he was taught at an early age to play the violin. When the Drakes came to the United States in 1810, he became second violinist in Bernard's Albany Theatre. Though an accomplished musician, he wanted to become an actor; and after making his debut as Edmund in *King Lear* on the Albany stage, he performed many supporting roles in the stock pieces of the day. He acted in all the plays managed by his father on the journey west and in the Kentucky theatres, but his musical ability forced him to spend much of his time directing stage orchestras and accompanying singers. As an actor he never ranked with his younger brother Alexander or his sister Julia; his first reviews in Louisville failed to draw the praise that was given to other members of Drake's troupe. Had he not been involved with stage music, he might have developed his acting talents at an earlier age. Ludlow describes young Samuel as a handsome, efficient, and kindhearted man but one who "soon fell into the company of men fond of high living and it did not take long to make him one of the same." He died in Cincinnati on July 24, 1826, at the age of thirty.[3]

The second son, Alexander, was born in 1798.[4] When the family moved to Boston, Alexander, at the age of thirteen, played the Prince of Wales in *Richard III*. Early in life he began to specialize in low comic roles, a popular line of business that required unusual talent. With his good singing voice and ready wit he developed this specialty to a marked degree and became known throughout the western circuits as an excellent low comedian and singer of comic songs. Few actors could surpass Alexander Drake in these parts—"country boys" or singing comedians.[5] He was not limited, however, to this specialty. Joe Cowell, a contemporary actor and one of Alexander's managers, states that Alexander could play Charles Surface in Sheridan's *School for Scandal* "much better than I have often seen it done by those who consider such characters their line of business."[6] Though troubled by deafness, a con-

---

[1] *Dramatic Life*, p. 365.
[2] Ibid.
[3] Ibid., pp. 363-64.
[4] Ibid., p. 364.
[5] Ibid.
[6] Joe Cowell, *Thirty Years Passed among the Players in England and America* (New York, 1884), pp. 85-86.

132 THE THEATRE IN EARLY KENTUCKY

dition which would seem fatal to an actor, Alexander assumed a variety of roles and managed to draw excellent reviews. He was always a hit with western audiences, especially when the time came for comic songs. It was not unusual for the audience to throw ten or twelve dollars on the stage during each of his singing acts.[7]

Alexander Drake's easygoing nature, however, was a hindrance to his managerial career in later years. Joe Cowell met him in 1829 in Cincinnati, where he had been sent by his father to manage the theatre for a season. Cowell recalls his first encounter with Alexander:

> I was making some inquiries of the barkeeper about the theatre, when a man about my own age and size, very shabby, very dirty, and very deaf, introduced himself as Alex Drake, the mgr. He curled his right hand round his ear, and in a courteous whisper, invited me to "take something." He was a kind, familiar, light-hearted creature, told me, with apparent glee, that he was over head and ears in debt to the co. and everybody else; and that that night he had given the use of the theatre and the performers had tendered their services to an old actor who expected a "meeting of his creditors"; but that he had been obliged to close the theatre for the simple reason that it wasn't *fashionable.*[8]

Old Drake was then in Frankfort waiting for Alexander and the company to rejoin him so that he could open the theatre there, but Alexander could not leave Cincinnati until "relieved by the insolvent law."[9] As early as 1822 Samuel Drake had turned over much of the management, especially in the areas bordering Kentucky, to his son. In 1822 Alexander managed engagements in Cincinnati, Nashville, and in Fayetteville, Arkansas. In the summer of 1822 he and his wife organized a company and played a short season at the "Albany Circus in front of the capitol."[10]

Alexander Drake married Frances Ann Denny. Their daugh-

[7] Ibid., p. 87.
[8] Ibid., p. 86.
[9] Ibid., p. 87.
[10] *Players of a Century*, p. 60.

ter, Julia, named after Alexander's sister, married Harry Chapman of showboat fame. The popular Chapman sisters, daughters of Harry and Julia Drake Chapman, were well-known variety performers throughout the West in later years. Alexander and Frances Drake also had three sons: Samuel Drake III, who became an actor; Colonel E. A. Drake of the United States Army; and Richard Drake, who was killed at the battle of Monterrey in the Mexican War.[11]

Frances Trollope's *Domestic Manners of the Americans* pays a distinguished tribute to the acting talents of Alexander Drake. Mrs. Trollope, who abhorred the tobacco-chewing, backwoods audiences she met in her western travels, found nothing but praise for the skills of Alexander Drake and his wife:

> Nothing could be more distinct than their line of acting, but the great versatility of their powers enabled them often to appear together. Her cast was the highest walk of tragedy, and his the broadest comedy; but yet, as Goldsmith says of his sister heroines, I have known them to change characters for a whole evening together, and have wept with him and laughed with her, as it was their will and pleasure to ordain. I think in his comedy he was superior to any actor I ever saw in the same parts, except Emery. Alexander Drake's comedy was like that of the French, who never appear to be acting at all; he was himself the comic being the author aimed at depicting. Let him speak whose words he would, from Shakespeare to Colman, it was impossible not to feel that half the fun was his own; he had, too, in a very high degree, the power that Fawcett possessed, of drawing tears by a sudden touch of natural feeling. His comic songs might have set the gravity of the judges and bishops together at defiance. Liston is great but Alexander was greater.[12]

Alexander Drake died in Cincinnati on February 10, 1830, at the age of thirty-two.[13] On hearing of his death, the Kentucky and Ohio Legislatures adjourned their sessions.[14]

[11] *Dramatic Life*, pp. 364-65.
[12] Frances Trollope, *Domestic Manners of the Americans*, ed. Donald Smalley (New York, 1949), p. 129.
[13] *Dramatic Life*, p. 364.
[14] George D. Ford, *These Were Actors* (New York, 1955), p. 168.

Samuel Drake's younger daughter, Julia, was born in 1800.[15] She was only fifteen at the time of the family trek to Kentucky, but with her natural talent and beauty she developed rapidly into a gifted performer. She was "a perfect specimen of the ancient Italian beauty,—dark hair and long, dark eyelashes, her eyes had a peculiarly happy, lively expression." Ludlow thought that Julia Drake had the greatest acting ability in the family; he believed that had she been trained in the eastern theatres, she would have attained as great a national reputation as did her famous daughter, Julia Dean.[16] Unlike her brother who excelled in low comedy, Julia became a splendid performer in high comedy as well as an actress in serious drama. Her portrayal of Lady Teazle in *The School for Scandal* was so excellently articulated that Ludlow described it as "musical, full, and joyous."[17] W. D. Adams's *Dictionary of the Drama* may be exaggerating in stating that Julia Drake "was the first native actress to electrify the western country,"[18] but she and Frances Ann Denny were the first celebrated actresses to develop their talents before western audiences. After Ludlow had performed with Julia Drake in Nashville during the Drakes' season there in 1822, he said her performances of Lady Racket in *Three Weeks after Marriage* and the Widow Cheerly in *The Soldier's Daughter* were the best delineations of the two roles that he had witnessed in fifty years.[19] Julia Drake married a Cincinnati merchant and banker named Fosdick who died a few years after their marriage. She had a son and a daughter by this marriage; the son, W. W. Fosdick, became a well-known western poet. Julia's second marriage was to Edwin Dean, an actor in New York. They had two children, Julia and Helen. Julia Dean became one of the country's leading actresses of the midcentury, not only in the western theatres, where she played for many seasons, but in the eastern theatres

---

[15] *Dramatic Life*, p. 365.
[16] Ibid.
[17] Ibid.
[18] W. Davenport Adams, *A Dictionary of the Drama* . . . (Philadelphia, 1905), p. 423.
[19] *Dramatic Life*, p. 240.

as well. Following in her mother's and grandfather's tradition, Julia Dean opened the new Louisville Theatre in 1846 after Samuel Drake's old theatre burned in 1843.[20] Julia Drake died in Duchess County, New York, in 1832.[21]

James G. Drake, the third son and youngest child of Samuel Drake, was born in England in 1802.[22] As a child he acted and sang in his father's troupe during the journey west, but after the family settled in Louisville he seldom accepted stage roles except to sing or to accompany singers with his guitar. Later he studied law but "never became prominent in the profession."[23] He married the daughter of Alexander Breckinridge, brother of James D. Breckinridge, a member of Congress from Louisville, 1821-1823. James Drake was a poet and a writer of such popular songs as "Beautiful Isle Where the Sun Goes Down," "Tom Breeze," and *"Parlez bas."*[24] James Drake, the last surviving child of Samuel Drake, died in Louisville on May 13, 1850.[25]

Although Frances Ann Denny was not related to the Drake family except through marriage, she was a member of the original Drake troupe and used the name Drake in establishing herself as the first theatre manageress in the West. She was born in Schenectady, New York, on November 6, 1797. After her family moved to Albany, she worked under Samuel Drake and came west with his troupe in 1815. She performed as a supporting juvenile actress with the Drake company until 1819, when she left Kentucky for engagements in the theatres of Montreal, Boston, and New York. In 1820 she appeared at the Park Theatre in New York in the popular comedy *Man and Wife* and afterward became a regular member of that company.

Alexander Drake visited the East in 1822, renewed his friend-

---

[20] "Early Days in Kentucky."
[21] *Dramatic Life*, p. 365.
[22] Ibid.
[23] Ibid.
[24] *History of Louisville*, 2: 329. Lewis Collins quotes *"Parlez bas"* in *History of Kentucky*, 2 vols. (Covington, Ky., 1882), 1: 564.
[25] Ibid.

ship with Frances Ann Denny, and married her in 1822 or 1823.[26] Returning to Kentucky, they worked as a team in managing the theatrical interests of Samuel Drake, Sr., who had made Louisville his home and who now limited much of his theatre work to that city. Using her married name as a stage name, Mrs. Alexander Drake became the organizer of the team and once again carried the magic name of Drake throughout Kentucky and into the surrounding areas of the West.

At the time of Alexander's death in 1830 Mrs. Drake was the most prominent person in western theatrical circles; in fact, she was referred to as "the Star of the West" until her reputation as an actress declined after 1836.[27] She married G. W. Cutter from Cincinnati, but the marriage ended in separation. During the 1830s and early 1840s Mrs. Drake made frequent trips to the East to play engagements there. In 1835 she appeared for the last time in New York as Bianca in *Fazio*.[28] After 1835 she managed the Louisville Theatre and performed leading roles with visiting stars there until the theatre was destroyed by fire in 1843. In October 1851, with her son-in-law and daughter, Mr. and Mrs. Harry Chapman, she operated another Louisville theatre, the Histrionic Temple, located on the site of the old Louisville Theatre.[29] For some time she owned a home in Covington, Kentucky, but after her retirement from the stage she moved to her father-in-law's farm in Oldham County. She died there on September 1, 1875.[30]

J. Stoddard Johnston provides the following information about Mrs. Drake:

> She was a very interesting woman, as well as an actress of mark. Col. R. T. Durrett has, among other souvenirs of her, two autograph letters, which give a fair insight into her merit as an actress and her station in society. The first is from Washington Irving, written in October, 1832, as a letter of introduction to Mr. William Jordan of London, in which, referring to Mrs.

[26] *DAB*, 5: 428.
[27] Ibid.
[28] *Dramatic Life*, p. 367.
[29] *Courier-Journal*, 5 February 1922.
[30] *DAB*, 5: 428.

Drake's professional merit, he says he has "seen her in the character of the 'Widow Cheerly' and 'Mary, the Maid of the Inn.' In both of them she appeared to me to equal the best of similar performers that I have lately seen on the London board." The second letter is from John Howard Payne, author of "Home, Sweet Home," written May 20, 1833, as Mrs. Drake was about to sail for Europe. It is addressed to Mrs. Winter, London, and among other complimentary things, says: "Mrs. Drake, who is one of the few Americans warmly praised by Mrs. Trollope, visits England with a view to a professional experiment in London. You may infer what her chances may be from what is said of her in the 'Travels' of the Duke of Saxe-Weimar. He calls her the 'Siddons of the West,' probably destined to become the Siddons of the world." Bernhard, Duke of Saxe-Weimar, here spoken of, arrived in Louisville, April 26, 1826, and gives the city a very favorable notice. He attended the theatre on the occasion of the benefit of Mrs. Drake, when two pieces were played, "Man and Wife," an English drama, and a farce called "Three Weeks After Marriage." He says: "The theatre was well filled, as Mrs. Drake was very much of a favorite with the ladies here. All the boxes were full of the fashionables of the place." Mrs. Trollope visited Louisville in the spring of 1828. Mrs. Drake played as a member of Drake's Company at intervals until 1840, taking the leading part in many dramas. Among others we note in the press of the day, "Dr. Faustus and the Devil," and the "News Letter," of July 27, 1839, stated that she closed the season on the 22nd with "Adrian and Orilla."[31]

Mrs. Trollope thought that Mrs. Drake's performance of Belvidera in Otway's *Venice Preserved* was, except for the portrayal of Mrs. Siddons, the best that she had ever seen.[32] It is interesting that Mrs. Trollope would compare Mrs. Drake with the great Mrs. Siddons since Mrs. Drake did win the titles "the Star of the West" and "the Siddons of the West." Joe Jefferson, a younger contemporary of Mrs. Drake, says that she was the leading tragic actress in America before the arrival of Charlotte Cushman: "She was an accomplished lady, and

[31] *History of Louisville*, 2: 328-29.
[32] Trollope, *Domestic Manners of the Americans*, p. 130.

during her whole life held an enviable position on and off the stage. When a boy of sixteen I acted with her the page Cyprian Gossamer in "Adrian and Orilla," she taught me the business of the part with great care, coming to the theatre an hour before rehearsal so as to go over the scenes with me before the actors assembled. She had a queenly bearing, and was, during her dramatic reign, undoubtedly the tragic muse of America.[33]

Almost twenty years after Frances Ann Denny acted her first role of Imma in *Adelgitha* at Canandaigua, New York, en route to Kentucky, she performed as a star in the same piece at the Park Theatre in New York. The critic described her as an "ornament to the American Stage" and praised her acting in both *Adelgitha* and *The Hunchback*.[34]

After Samuel Drake had finished his first season in Lexington in November 1816, he moved on to Frankfort and Louisville. However, his record from 1817 to 1820, especially in the two latter towns, is incomplete. The scattered issues of the Frankfort newspapers from 1816 to 1820 offer only three theatrical notices and only one performance announcement, on December 30, 1819, of *The Heir at Law* and *Timour the Tartar*. Louisville's newspaper notices in 1817 are limited to five brief listings of nine performances in March and April; of the nine plays announced by Drake during that Louisville season, James Kenny's farce *Turn Out* was the only new one. Ludlow mentions the names of ten plays for the 1817 Frankfort engagement, but he says nothing concerning the offerings in Louisville during the same season.[35] All the plays listed by Ludlow in Frankfort had been performed in Kentucky in past seasons.

On Monday, March 3, 1817, the *Louisville Correspondent* announced that Drake had opened the theatre on the preceding Monday; however, previous issues had failed to announce the opening plays. After giving Drake the usual polite welcome,

[33] Joseph Jefferson, *The Autobiography of Joseph Jefferson* (New York, 1889–1890), p. 415.
[34] George C. D. Odell, *Annals of the New York Stage*, vol. 3 (New York, 1927), p. 667.
[35] *Dramatic Life*, p. 102.

"the return of old friends is at all times pleasing to us," the writer criticized Drake for failing to bring to Louisville two new actors engaged in Lexington, Joshua Collins and Aaron Phillips. Drake was reminded that the citizens of Louisville had been liberal in their support of him during his first season. Phillips did appear later in the Louisville season and played the leading role of Young Norval in *Douglas* on March 22.[36] Phillips, who joined Drake in Frankfort, was a Jewish actor who had performed at New York's Park Theatre in 1815 and whose name had appeared in the Philadelphia and Charleston theatres before his arrival in Kentucky.[37] After one season with Drake Phillips joined Ludlow on the barnstorming trip to Nashville. On March 15 the *Louisville Correspondent* announced the debut on March 17 of John Savage, Drake's other recruit in 1817, as Rolla in *Pizarro*. Savage also left Drake after one season; like Ludlow and Phillips, he found his way to New Orleans in 1819, where he and his wife performed in *Venice Preserved, The Day after the Wedding,* and *The Romp.* His notices there stated that he was from Boston.[38]

During the summer of 1817 Ludlow and a few other actors engaged by Drake formed a commonwealth company, as they called it, to take the drama to Nashville and other points in the South where no professional stage performances had taken place. The small group included Ludlow, his fiancée, Mr. and Mrs. John Vaughan, Henry Vaughan, Aaron Phillips, and a musician named Bainbridge. (John Vaughan had recently married the daughter of a prominent Frankfort physician named Newberry.) Exactly how this small group produced plays while traveling to Nashville is not known, but they arranged for a wagon and horses and left Louisville in June. They performed *The Weathercock* and *The Village Lawyer* for two nights in the ballroom in Elizabethtown, Kentucky, and also gave performances in Russellville, Kentucky.[39]

[36] *Louisville Correspondent,* 22 March 1817.
[37] *Dramatic Life,* pp. 324-25.
[38] Nellie Smither, *A History of the English Theatre in New Orleans* (New York, 1967), p. 17.
[39] *Dramatic Life,* pp. 108-10.

Before Drake's Lexington engagement beginning the last of August 1817, he took his regular company to Paris, Kentucky, for a week of performances starting on Friday, August 15, with *Turn Out* and *Sylvester Daggerwood*. The company performed on Saturday, August 16, and on Monday, Wednesday, Friday, and Saturday of the following week. The *Western Citizen*, August 13, announced the name of only one other play during the Paris engagement, *The Quaker*, performed on Saturday, August 23.

Fortunately, Drake's 1817 engagement in Lexington was a lengthy one that received regular advertisement in the best-preserved newspapers in the state. That Drake was making a strong bid to win the Lexington audiences is obvious from his announcement in the *Gazette*, August 23, 1817:

> Mr. Drake respectfully informs the Ladies and Gentlemen of Lexington, that having completed the various improvements in the interior of the theatre, the house will be open for a short season immediately; and again he pledges himself to an indulgent public, that no effort on his part will be wanting to prove himself deserving of their patronage.
>
> A few *season tickets* (transferable) will be issued. The Box Office will in future be kept in the lower end of the theatre, and will be opened every day on which a performance is to take place, from four o'clock in the afternoon until nine at night.—a *Coffee Room* in the rear of the boxes will be provided, and also a side room with confections and other refreshments.

Offering only one season rather than two, as he had done the preceding year, Drake opened Usher's theatre on Thursday, August 28, 1817, with *Speed the Plough* and "other entertainments." During the previous season in Lexington he had performed from May to July, and he had learned from this experience that the summer season in Kentucky was no time for drama production. In the August 27 *Reporter* Drake emphasized again that he had "spared neither pains nor expense to render the house commodious and comfortable." The Lexington newspapers announced twenty-eight plays offered on sixteen nights from August 27 through November 15, 1817; again, however, they failed to announce all the performances. The company, playing two or three times a week, advertised their Saturday productions mainly, with a few scattered Wednesday announcements recorded in the *Reporter*. Colman's operatic romance *The Forty Thieves*, for example, had two notices, but the *Gazette* announcement on Saturday, October 18, mentioned that the piece had already "been twice performed in our theatre, the present week, to crowded and brilliant houses."

The company presented a variety of pieces with nine new comedies, farces, musicals, and comic operas: *The Forty Thieves*, Mrs. Inchbald's sentimental play *Such Things Are, or The Noble Philanthropist*, Susannah Rowson's patriotic drama *Americans in Algiers*, Charles Lamb's farce *Mr. H, or Beware of a Bad Name*, Prince Hoare's comic opera *Three and the Deuce, or Which Is Which?*, Cibber and VanBrugh's comedy *The Provoked Husband*, Allingham's farce properly called *'Tis All a Farce*, Bickerstaffe's comic opera *Love in a Village*, and an anonymous farce listed as *Past Ten O'clock, and a Rainy Night*.[40]

Few items of interest appeared in the newspapers concerning the productions, the actors, or the theatre management. On October 18 the *Gazette* announced that *The Forty Thieves* had been received with "universal applause" and that Drake had performed it with justice. According to the reviewer, who had seen the play in Baltimore, it "was never done better." The scenery was splendid and the actors were suited to their roles. Blisset, the "inimitable" actor, always acted his characters according to Hamlet's advice "suiting the action to the word." Alexander Drake acted the role of Ali Baba with "spirit and correctness," and James Drake also performed with spirit in the role of Ganem. Miss Julia Drake performed the part of Morgiana with a "modest representation"; Miss Denny and Samuel Drake, Jr., "acquitted themselves respectably." In fact, the entire production of *The Forty Thieves* drew praises from the critic, who thought it reflected "credit on the theatricals

[40] *Gazette*, 6, 13, 20 September, 11, 18, 25 October, 8 November; *Reporter*, 1 October 1817.

of the West." He continued by praising Drake's efforts and emphatically stating that Drake deserved a "liberal patronage!"

Benefit performances began on October 29 with *Pizarro* and *Catherine and Petruchio*, the benefit for Samuel Drake, Jr. Blisset took his benefit on November 1 with *He Would Be a Soldier*. Mr. and Mrs. Savage from the Philadelphia Theatre announced their benefit for Tuesday, November 4, but did not announce their plays. Alexander Drake took a benefit on November 8 with *Three and the Deuce*. Another notice in the November 8 *Gazette* concerned the theatre's music which had been greatly improved by the acquisition of a violinist who had played a solo several nights before, "the finest ever performed on that instrument in our orchestra."

At the close of the season the *Gazette*, November 15, 1817, printed a tribute to Samuel Drake, Sr., on the occasion of his benefit:

> Mr. Drake, as an actor, will always be seen with great pleasure. Correctness of style, and great definition of character are always conspicuous in his acting.—As a Manager, he has proved, by his skill and ability, his qualifications for the task confided to him. By persevering industry, and his own liberality, he has snatched our theatre from the obscurity, and gained a complete sanction for the establishment; creating surprize in our eastern friends, who travel into this state and witness it. Such a man is deserving the need of public munificence, and ought not, fellow citizens, to have empty boxes seen on this occasion.

An announcement in the *Western Spy* of a benefit performance for Mrs. Turner in Cincinnati on Friday, January 31, 1817, was the first bit of information concerning the Turners since their departure from Lexington in the fall of 1815. Apparently they had joined the Cincinnati amateurs to organize a theatrical season there sometime in 1816. The benefit announced on January 31 was not, however, the end of the 1817 season in Cincinnati; Mrs. Turner acted again on February 21, March 14, July 11, September 26, and November 21. The Turners produced *The Castle Spectre* and *Of Age Tomorrow* on January 31, with Mrs. Turner acting the role of Angela in *The Castle Spectre*. Osmond was played by "a gentleman of Cincinnati," "his first appearance for several years." Advertising as "the last night but one," the Turners presented for Stall's benefit on Friday, February 21, *Pizarro* and a pantomime, *Harlequin in the Moon*. On Friday, March 14, "positively the very last night," the patrons of the drama saw *The Merchant of Venice, or The Inexorable Jew* (an interesting but unheard-of second title for Shakespeare's play). It was followed on the program by *Love Laughs at Locksmiths* and a farewell address written by "a gentleman of Cincinnati." Mrs. Turner played Portia in *The Merchant of Venice* and Collins acted Shylock. Collins, who had performed with Drake during the Lexington and Frankfort seasons of 1816-1817, had chosen to join Turner in Cincinnati in February 1817.

The theatre in Cincinnati reopened on July 11 with an address by Mrs. Turner to the patrons of the drama, followed by a performance of *Barbarossa* and *Darkness Visible*. On September 26 Mrs. Turner received another benefit from the Cincinnati Thespians and the "Harmonical Society" with a production of *Oroonoko, or The Noble Slave*, a dramatization by Thomas Southerne of Mrs. Aphra Behn's novel. At the end of the play Mrs. Turner recited "Eliza, or The Battle of Minden Plain." Mrs. Turner's last appearance in Cincinnati during the 1817 visit took place on Friday, November 21, with C. R. Marturin's play *Bertram*. She acted Imogene, and Lewis, who joined Drake the following year, played Bertram. Lewis concluded the evening's entertainment with imitations of the celebrated actors Cooke, Cooper, Fennell, Duff, and Wood.[41]

Ludlow, who with a small group had left Drake in 1817, decided that to perform for another season in Nashville he would need more actors. He and Phillips started by horseback from Nashville to Cincinnati sometime in August 1817, making the journey in about a week. Ludlow does not give the date for his arrival in Cincinnati, but he mentions that the Turners

[41] *Western Spy*, 31 January, 21 February, 14 March, 11 July, 26 September, 21 November 1817.

were then having benefits at the close of their season. Here again Ludlow is mistaken with his performance dates. If he visited Cincinnati in time for Mrs. Turner's benefit on September 26, he could not possibly have been back in Nashville for his announced September 1 opening. Ludlow was unimpressed with Turner's organization in Cincinnati, but one should bear in mind that he was seldom impressed with competing stage troupes: "We found in Cincinnati a small company performing under the management of Mr. Turner, familiarly known as 'Billy Turner'; but owing to a long term of bad business he had not been able to pay the salaries of his actors, and consequently there was nothing but complaint and insubordination among them." Ludlow and Phillips performed with Mrs. Turner in her benefit performance *The Honeymoon* (a play not announced in the Cincinnati newspapers) to an overflowing house, in a theatre described by Ludlow as a "small, ill-contrived place they called a theatre." This converted building, located close to Fourth and Main streets, was erected on a rising piece of ground, a place that "was by a long flight of rough plank steps, up which an audience had to ascend and descend, at the imminent peril of their limbs and life." If Ludlow was displeased with the company and the theatre in Cincinnati, he was compensated by the acting of Mrs. Turner, who drew his praises for her performance of Juliana in *The Honeymoon*. She "was easy and lady-like in her deportment on the stage and showed considerable professional culture."[42]

Turner closed out his season in Cincinnati after his usual run of bad luck, having lost some of his small group to Ludlow who took them back with him to Nashville. Not one to surrender easily to such misfortunes, Turner arrived in the frontier town of St. Louis in January 1818 with a "Company of players" who performed in the courthouse and the Green Tree Tavern. Vos, who had last been heard from in Louisville with Drake's company, joined Turner in St. Louis for the first professional engagement in that city in 1818. They presented *Bertram, The Mock Doctor, Isabella, 'Tis All a Farce, The*

[42] *Dramatic Life*, pp. 115-16.

Road to Ruin, George Barnwell, Children in the Wood, Tekeli, Henry IV, Richard III, and *The Intriguing Valet.*[43]

Again, there are almost no newspaper records for theatrical activity in Frankfort and Louisville in 1818, a dearth caused not only by missing newspapers but also by missing stage notices in extant newspapers. However, the Lexington newspapers once again preserved Drake's record in Kentucky by advertising another long and successful Lexington engagement in 1818. If Drake had any apprehension concerning his business relationship with Luke Usher, he showed nothing but enthusiasm in his opening announcement in the *Gazette* on Friday, August 21, 1818:

LEXINGTON THEATRE

The Manager respectfully announces the opening of the theatre for a short season, which will take place as soon as the reinforcements, under the escort of Mr. Alexander, arrives. He begs leave to assure the Ladies and Gentlemen of Lexington, that the house will continue to be conducted with that strict attention which heretofore has obtained the distinguished patronage of his friends and the suffrage of a candid public. A selection of new DRAMAS of approved worth, of moral and political tendency, are in his contemplation, and which will be supported by performers of excellent capacities. Neither expense nor pains will be spared to lift the Drama from the chilling obscurity of a barbarous epoch, and to place it on the pinnacle of national respect, worthy of a free, unprejudiced people, whose labors to enlighten and cultivate the field of science, are so eminently conspicuous.

No one could accuse Samuel Drake of not having a flair for words. It is understandable that he enjoyed adding his own second titles to plays.

Lexington's 1818 season opened on Friday, September 4, with *Macbeth* and *The Weathercock*. Palmer Fisher, the brother-in-law of Samuel Drake, had been recruited by Alexander Drake and began his starring career in the western theatre in Lexington as Macbeth to Mrs. Groshon's Lady

[43] *The Theatre on the Frontier,* pp. 22-26.

Macbeth. Fisher and his wife had managed provincial theatres in England and had acted supporting roles at Drury Lane as early as 1805 in the same company with Collins and Bland.[44] On August 7, 1818, about a month before he acted Macbeth in Lexington, Fisher submitted to the *Gazette* a letter of recommendation written for him by the renowned English actor Edmund Kean: "I hereby recommend my worthy friend, Mr. Palmer Fisher, to the particular notice of any American gentleman with whom he may take his passage to the United States; feeling conscious that his talents as an Actor (which were held in highest estimation at the Theatre Royal, Drury Lane) and qualities as a Man need only be witnessed to obtain him the admiration and esteem of the liberal sons of Columbia. March 12, 1818." During his first season in Lexington Fisher went unnoticed, as did all the other players except William Jones, who drew praises for his comic talent. That Fisher was not a tremendously impressive actor is obvious from the general review of the season. On October 28 a critic for the *Reporter* stated that Jones would be at home in certain roles, as would Alexander Drake, but that Fisher as Reuben Glenroy in *Town and Country* "will be tolerable well." Ludlow described Fisher as having "a heavy, dull face, perfectly void of any expression."[45] Fisher acted for several seasons with Drake, moved back to the eastern theatres, and died in Boston in 1827. His wife, a talented actress in character roles, made her home in Philadelphia until 1852.[46]

Other new actors who joined Drake in 1818 were Mrs. Groshon, Mrs. Mongin, Jones, and Lewis. The name Phillips also occurs in two announcements of that season; this may have been the same Aaron J. Phillips who went with Ludlow to Nashville the preceding year. Mrs. Belinda Groshon, an excellent actress in the early western theatre,[47] was born in England. She was known as Mrs. Goldson until her appearance at the Park Theatre in New York in 1813.[48] After her western

[44] *Times* (London), 1 January 1805.
[45] *Dramatic Life*, p. 189.
[46] Ibid.
[47] *Chronology of the American Stage*, p. 63.

engagement with Drake in 1818 she joined Collins and Jones in Cincinnati in June the following year. She died in Cincinnati on January 31, 1822.[49] The October 16, 1818, *Gazette* praised her in the only detailed review of the season:

> We believe that without a dissenting vote, the public has awarded to this lady the praise of being the best actress that ever appeared on the western stage, and the writer can say with truth, and with pleasure, that having witnessed the displays of dramatic talents in the Atlantic states for many years past, he has seen no lady more able, more completely at home, in the characters she represents, than Mrs. Groshon. One of the best means which we may cause theatrical exhibitions to be improved, is to exercise a spirit of discernment and discrimination in patronising genuine merit. Such we find in Mrs. Groshon; and it is sincerely hoped that the friends of the drama, ladies as well as gentlemen, will evince their usual tastes and respect for talents on the occasion of the benefit of that excellent actress, which is fixed for Saturday evening.
>
> **W. O.**

The other important actor recruited by Alexander Drake in 1818 was William Jones, who became a well-known player of old men's roles throughout the West and South.[50] After making his western debut with Drake, he joined Joshua Collins in managing the Cincinnati theatre on June 21, 1819.[51] Born in Maryland in 1781, Jones acted in Richmond, Philadelphia, and New York before moving west. He managed companies in Nashville, St. Louis, Lexington, and Cincinnati before leaving the western stage to manage the Arch Street Theatre in Philadelphia. He died in New York on December 1, 1841.[52] The *Reporter* of October 28, 1818, complimented him highly before his benefit performance that evening: "To those who have witnessed Mr. Jones' exertions in the drama, it is unnecessary to

---

48 *Annals of the New York Stage*, 2: 419, 457.

49 T. Alliston Brown, *A History of the New York Stage from the First Performance in 1732 to 1901*, 3 vols. (New York, 1870), 1: 152.

50 *Chronology of the American Stage*, p. 81.

51 *Western Spy*, 19 June 1819.

52 *Chronology of the American Stage*, p. 81.

say how much he has contributed to the amusement and delight of the friends of theatrical exhibitions. The reputation he acquired in New York has followed him to Lexington."
Mrs. Victor F. Mongin and James O. Lewis, strolling players recruited by Alexander Drake in 1818, were unknown actors who made their western debuts in Lexington. Mrs. Mongin performed with Drake until 1822; she is listed as a member of Caldwell's company in New Orleans in 1824.[53] Lewis acted for two seasons with Drake before returning to New York.

Although Drake announced his 1818 Lexington season as a short one, he produced over forty plays in more than twenty performances. Again he performed on Wednesdays and Fridays, but he failed to publicize many of the Wednesday productions. *The School of Reform*, for example, was announced while in rehearsal but was not advertised in the regular notices. Drake carried out his promise to bring "a selection of new dramas" to Lexington, producing five new offerings during the season: Colman's melodrama *The Iron Chest, or A Mysterious Murder*, Pocock's sentimental melodrama *The Magpie and the Maid, or Who's the Thief?*, Knight's comic opera *The Turnpike Gate*, Lewis's melodrama *Alfonso, King of Castile*, and Murphy's farce *The Old Maid*.[54]

A glance at three of Drake's new pieces reveals that although he desired "to lift the Drama from the chilling obscurity of a barbarous epoch," the new plays were of the same melodramatic, sentimental mould of past years. *The Iron Chest*, a typical stock melodrama of intrigue, uses the traditional villain with an unsavory past who almost ruins the young hero; the hero is saved by evidence of the villain's guilt discovered in an old iron chest. In *The Magpie and the Maid* an ill-treated, poverty-stricken heroine is accused of stealing a spoon. After much sentimental, childish dialogue, all is put right by the discovery that a magpie is the thief. Monk Lewis's *Alfonso, King of Castile* is another of his intense melodramas of revenge.

[53] Smither, *History of the English Theatre in New Orleans*, p. 40.
[54] *Reporter*, 16, 23 September, 14 October, 4 November 1818; *Gazette*, 23 October 1818.

That Drake had organized an effective theatrical operation after two years in the West is apparent from the variety of drama presented during the 1818 Lexington engagement. Only two plays of the more than forty announced had second showings: *The Magpie and the Maid* and *The Forty Thieves.* In addition to the stock pieces Drake presented *Macbeth, Henry IV, The School for Scandal,* and *She Stoops to Conquer.*[55]

On Friday, November 20, 1818, the *Gazette* published the only complete cast list announced during the Lexington engagement:

The Soldier's Daughter

Governor Heartall	Jones
Frank Heartall	Fisher
Young Malfort	Douglas
Old Malfort	S. Drake
Captain Woodly	Lewis
Mr. Ferrit	Alexander Drake
Timothy Quaint	———
Widow Cheerly	Mrs. Groshon
Mrs. Malfort	Julia Drake
Mrs. Fidget	Mrs. Lewis
Susan	Mrs. Mongin
Julia	Miss Fisher

Among other bits of newspaper information concerning Drake's 1818 season in Lexington is a notice that the theatre doors opened at six-thirty for the performance at seven-thirty. For his benefit on October 14 Fisher delivered as a "prelude" "A Grand Exordium on Free Masonry in full clothing of a Royal Arch Mason. To commence with the Mason's song 'No Sect in the World Can with Masona Compare.' " In *Isabella* Fisher acted Biron, Jones played Sampson, and Mrs. Groshon took the leading part of Isabella. In *Alfonso* Samuel Drake played Orsino, Jones acted Caesario, Mrs. Groshon performed Ottilia, and Julia Drake represented Amelrosa. Alexander Drake,

[55] *Gazette,* 4 September, 6 November 1818; *Reporter,* 4, 11 November 1818.

following his usual line, played the comic lead in *Sylvester Daggerwood*.[56]

The 1818-1819 theatrical season not only established Drake's domination of the Kentucky stage but also saw the development of drama production in many other areas throughout the West and South. Ludlow had taken the drama to Nashville, Natchez, and New Orleans in 1817 and 1818.[57] Turner had moved in 1817 from Cincinnati to St. Louis, where he and Vos began the first professional engagement in that city early in 1818.[58] In March 1819 the Turners were acting in New Orleans after having performed in almost every community west of the Allegheny Mountains. On June 21, 1819, Joshua Collins and William Jones formed a managerial partnership in a Cincinnati venture which began in a room at the corner of Columbia and Walnut streets; the *Western Spy* of June 19, 1819, described the room as "having been fitted for the purpose of dramatic representation." The same notice announced the opening performance, *Douglas* and *Fortune's Frolic*, and the employment of several actors who had been with Drake in Lexington the year before: Mrs. Groshon, Lewis, Mrs. Mongin, and Jones.

Although Drake never managed to gain control of the Lexington Theatre, he purchased both the Frankfort and the Louisville theatre properties prior to the 1819 season. He was busy remodeling both theatres in 1818 and 1819—the one in Frankfort before the December 1818 engagement and the one in Louisville sometime before the March 1819 opening.[59] Apparently both the Frankfort and Louisville theatres had been poorly maintained since their construction in 1808 and 1811.

Announcing the opening in Frankfort for "about the 1st. of Dec. Next," Drake described the renovation of the theatre in the *Argus of Western America* on November 20, 1818:

[56] *Reporter*, 14 October 1818; *Gazette*, 23, 16, 30 October 1818.
[57] Smither, *History of the English Theatre in New Orleans*, p. 15.
[58] *The Theatre on the Frontier*, p. 19.
[59] John J. Weisert, "The First Decade of Sam Drake's Louisville Theatre," *Filson Club History Quarterly* 39 (October 1965): 289.

Mr. Drake, respectfully informs his friends, and the public in general, that his establishment will commence the annual season on or before the 1st of Dec. next.

I. Considerable alterations
   A. Barrs before held at back of pit, are by a new flight of steps removed into parlour beneath it—egress at close of performance.
   B. The gallery, too small last season—new supports by 4 columns—side wings if that side of house opened for more room.
   C. Part of pit thrown under boxes for same reason.
II. New professors and ladies and gentlemen of excellence. New pieces added, "means—amusement, the object, instruction."

Unfortunately this notice, repeated on November 27, and one other, announcing a tax of ten dollars levied by the Frankfort Trustees against the theatre manager, are the only Frankfort stage announcements printed in 1818. That Drake owned the Frankfort property is certain for on July 17, 1821, he borrowed $1,650 from the Bank of Kentucky by mortgaging the Frankfort Theatre property on Broadway and St. Clair streets.[60] Samuel Drake gave the Frankfort property to his only living son, James, on August 10, 1846, "for love and affection"[61] James Drake sold the property at "Broadway and St. Clair Streets, where the old theatre was erected and now stands," to Jacob and Philip Swigert on October 18, 1847, for $3,000.[62]

Except for two conflicting statements—Henrico McMurtrie's criticism that the old Louisville Theatre was little better than a barn and Mann Butler's remark in Louisville's first city *Directory* that the theatre was a small establishment—little is known about the structure of the theatre before Drake remodeled it in 1818. The building, constructed on lot 215 on the north side of Jefferson Street sometime between 1806 and 1808, belonged to John C. Beeler, who paid Samuel Beeler

[60] Franklin County Deed Book 1 (Frankfort, Ky.), p. 354.
[61] Ibid., Book 2, p. 312.
[62] Ibid., p. 354.

$2,000 for the property on September 8, 1806.[63] On May 1, 1812, Beeler deeded three-fifths of the lot (the theatre portion) to John Gwathmey; John and Ann Gwathmey sold this portion of the lot to Levi Tyler for $3,500 on August 21, 1816.[64] (The block on Jefferson Street was divided into four lots, each measuring half an acre and each having 105 feet of frontage.[65]) Hence Levi Tyler owned the theatre property at the time of Drake's arrival in Louisville during the 1816 season. The exact date of Drake's purchase of the property from Tyler is not recorded, nor is his purchase of the Frankfort property; but Ludlow recalls that "Mr. Drake was quite successful during the first ten or twelve years of his Kentucky career, and during that time bought the building in Frankfort of which the theatre was a portion."[66] Drake apparently owned the Louisville Theatre until its destruction by fire in 1843.[67]

The extent of Drake's refurbishing of the Louisville Theatre during the latter part of 1818 is not known, but a description of the theatre by Colonel John Thompson Gray, recorded by J. Stoddard Johnston, reveals that in 1825 it was much improved over the 1808 "miserable concern hardly fit to be attended":

Drake's old Louisville theatre was a very creditable one, and had some features not excelled by its successors. It had a row of private boxes occupying the whole front of what is now the dress circle, as in the French Opera House in New Orleans. They were closed in the rear, having doors for entrance and open in front. The second tier was open and corresponded to the latter day dress circle, while the third was low priced as now. The pit was not the choice place, as now, but was occupied by men, veteran theatre-goers and critics. The theatre was lighted with a grand chandelier, swung from the dome, and with side lights, all of sperm candles. As he expresses it,

[63] Jefferson County Deed Book 8 (Louisville, Ky.), pp. 27, 517.
[64] Ibid., Book K, pp. 280-82.
[65] Weisert, "The First Decade of Sam Drake's Louisville Theatre," p. 287.
[66] *Dramatic Life*, p. 363.
[67] John J. Weisert, "Beginnings of the Kentucky Theatre Circuit," *Filson Club History Quarterly* 34 (July 1960): 283.

there never was a dripping candle. This was in keeping with all of Drake's appointments, the decorations of the theatre being in harmonious colors and every adjunct tastefully adjusted.[68]

Despite the flattering description offered by Colonel Gray, the theatre had its limitations before further improvements were made in 1829-1830. Duke Bernhard of Saxe-Weimar Eisenach, who saw a production of *Man and Wife* and *Three Weeks after Marriage* at the Louisville Theatre on April 27, 1826, described it as having quite a small proscenium, "a confined pit, a simple row of boxes, and a gallery."[69] The *Louisville Directory for the Year 1832*, quoting Mann Butler's *Outline of the Origin and Settlement of Louisville in Kentucky*, states that Louisville's remodeled theatre (after 1830) measured 102 feet in length, 52 feet in width, and approximately 34 in height. It could seat about 700 people. Butler continues with the information that the former house was "taken down, and the present handsome establishment erected by Mr. Drake, under the designation of the City Theatre."[70] According to John J. Weisert, however, the building was not "taken down," but the interior was renovated and enlarged.[71] McMurtrie's description of Drake's theatre agrees essentially with the one in the city *Directory*, except for the seating capacity, which McMurtrie estimates as 800. Ludlow remembered correctly that the building belonged to a man named Tyler and that it burned to the ground on May 21, 1843. He added that Drake had no insurance on the property, "in which he had invested most of his hard earnings of years."[72]

If Drake had experienced difficulty with his 1818 season in Louisville, he corrected the problem with an organized, lengthy engagement in his redecorated Louisville Theatre in 1819. Not only did he produce an excellent program of plays

[68] *History of Louisville*, 2: 329.

[69] Bernhard, Duke of Saxe-Weimar Eisenach, *Travels through North America, during the Years 1825 and 1826*, 2 vols. (Philadelphia, 1828), 2: 133.

[70] Quoted in *Louisville Directory for the Year 1832* (Louisville, Ky., 1832), p. 139.

[71] Weisert, "The First Decade of Sam Drake's Louisville Theatre," p. 304.

[72] *Dramatic Life*, pp. 89, 573.

from March 1 through June 5, 1819, but he also drew from the newspapers more detailed criticism and comment than at any other time in early western stage production. Drake attempted to perform three times each week, but either he failed to maintain this schedule or the press failed to announce all his productions. Some reviews mention performances which were not announced in the regular theatrical notices. No notices appeared from March 20 to March 26 and from March 28 to April 15, but on several occasions the newspapers printed theatrical notices three times in one week. Though the season opened on Monday, March 1, no announcement of the opening play appeared in the Louisville theatrical notices. The 1819 Louisville record shows that the company produced forty dramatic and musical pieces in twenty-two performances. Drake presented only five new offerings during the season: *The Apostate* by Richard L. Sheil, *The Belle's Stratagem* by Hannah Cowley, *Alexander the Great* by Nathaniel Lee, *Laugh When You Can* by Frederick Reynolds, and *Midas*, Kane O'Hara's burletta. In addition to the regular plays and musical entertainment provided by the company Drake introduced a musical concert conducted by A. P. Heinrich, a German musician who had performed with Drake in Lexington in 1817.[73]

A summary of the critical reviews, most of which were directed to the leading players, shows considerable differences of opinion concerning their talents. On March 6 a reporter praised Palmer Fisher for his interpretation of Macbeth, especially in the dagger scene, where he "portrayed the various workings of a half formed villain." Mrs. Groshon, as Lady Macbeth, gave the audience "an excellent piece of acting from beginning to end." Sam Drake, Jr., showed much improvement as Macduff: "Should he continue to study correct models of good acting, we shall hail him as an actor of no ordinary merit, and one who will

---

[73] This account of Drake's 1819 Louisville season (as well as several other documentations in this book) comes from Dr. John J. Weisert, who kindly donated his notes from the Louisville newspapers. He used some of the material in these notes in "The First Decade of Sam Drake's Louisville Theatre," p. 287. He also lists the productions of the 1819 season in his unpublished manuscript "The Curtain Rose."

do honor to our state." On the same program Mrs. Lewis's portrayal of the leading role in *The Old Maid* was described as "equal to any in the U.S.; it was a rich feast of wit."[74] Fisher received praise for his portrayal of Young Rapid in *A Cure for the Heart Ache*. Alexander's Nabob was "just what it ought to have been," and Jones performed "very well" as Old Rapid. According to the critic, Jones had resented an earlier review criticizing his acting of Bertram in *The Foundling of the Forest*. The critic responded, "We shall only observe that *in this* country, the liberty of the Press is as free and unrestrained as the liberty of speech." Julia Drake played Ella Vortex in *A Cure for the Heart Ache* with "her usual correctness and elegance." Lewis received criticism for not knowing his lines in *The Foundling of the Forest*, and Mrs. Groshon was encouraged to speak louder in the same play.[75] The *Louisville Public Advertiser* took Fisher to task for his acting in *Richard III*:

> The character of Richard is very uncompromising. We cannot expect Cooper's varying and striking expression from everyone, nor can a naturally monotonous voice be expected to produce a shaded effect. We can expect procission and faithfulness to the text.
>
> The gentleman who impersonated the Duke on Saturday evening did not give the part the befitting stamp—we have understood he has been conversant with some of the veterans of the stage and would have expected him to have emulated their example.

Mrs. Groshon's acting in *Richard III* was classified as "frigid"; nothing that she had done all season was as "imperfect" as her portrayal of the queen.[76] Alexander and Julia Drake always received compliments on their acting. Samuel Drake, Jr., did well with some parts and poorly in others, and Jones performed better in comedy than in serious drama. Mrs. Mongin was adequate but needed to speak with more volume.

While Drake was managing this successful engagement in

[74] *Louisville Public Advertiser*, 6 March 1819 (Weisert's unpublished notes).
[75] Ibid., 13 March 1819 (Weisert's unpublished notes).
[76] Ibid., 10 April 1819 (Weisert's unpublished notes).

Louisville, Luke Usher was experiencing adversity in Lexington. In March 1819 a fire destroyed the jail, Blount's grocery, and Usher's Tavern, The Sign of the Ship. Charles Staples asserts that as a result of this disaster Usher gave the Kentucky Circuit to Samuel Drake and a mortgage was made on the Lexington Theatre to Robert Wickliffe.[77] A mortgage was recorded in the courthouse, as Staples says, but Usher did not give the Kentucky Circuit to Drake. Despite his ailing financial condition, Usher was not finished with the theatrical business. On October 14, 1819, he advertised in the *Gazette* for a manager to operate his Lexington Theatre:

This building, large and capacious, is situated on Water and Spring streets, and for years past it has been occupied for theatrical displays in Lexington. It has recently received inside embellishments, to the amount of *two thousand dollars* in value.

The extent of the population of the town and neighborhood; the fine literary taste of those who constitute theatrical audiences; the liberality of the trustees in not imposing a tax on companies; and the distinguished encouragement the institution has heretofore received, renders Lexington, as it regards Dramatic exhibitions, the ATHENS of the west. The building will hold an audience capable of yielding 6 or 700 dollars a night. The undersigned, being at this time the sole proprietor, offers the above described Theatre to Let on reasonable terms to any genteel company who may apply to him first. An Eastern company, on their way out, will find encouragement at Pittsburgh, Cincinnati, Lexington upon their arrival, Frankfort and Louisville—as well as at many of the smaller towns in Ohio and Kentucky.

Luke Usher, Lexington, April 9, 1819.

That Drake would have "encouraged" a visiting eastern company in Frankfort or Louisville is doubtful. As we have seen, Drake had acquired the Louisville and Frankfort theatres before 1819 and thus controlled two-thirds of the Kentucky Circuit before Usher mortgaged his Lexington Theatre; no doubt

[77] Charles Staples, *History of Pioneer Lexington* (Lexington, Ky., 1939), p. 10.

Usher's repeated attempts to sell or lease his theatre and Drake's acquisition of the theatres in Frankfort and Louisville were not just coincidental. Usher apparently failed to recruit an eastern company, for Drake was back in Lexington in the fall of 1819 for a brief visit. Although Drake performed occasionally in Lexington in later years, he was unable to develop the theatrical program there. Other troupes visited Lexington after 1819, but the city never regained its leadership in western stage production. Usher did not lose his theatre until November 8, 1825, when it was sold at public auction as a result of a suit filed by the same Robert Wickliffe who held the mortgage. According to the *Reporter* of September 5, 1825, Usher lost the suit and was forced to sell his theatre.

The short season announced by Drake in Lexington during the fall of 1819 consisted of two productions, *The Heir at Law* and *The Adopted Child* on September 3 and *Timour the Tartar* on September 8.[78] Drake's failure to produce a complete season may have been influenced by Usher's advertising his theatre for lease at the same time Drake announced his season. Drake joined forces with West's Melodramatic Company to produce Monk Lewis's spectacular equestrian drama, *Timour the Tartar*. The combined efforts of West's live horses and Drake's actors resulted in a novel production of a sort not witnessed before on the western stage. Not only were West's horses "well-trained and splendid in appearance," but Drake's performers also drew compliments from the critics. Fisher as Timour was praised in the September 10 *Gazette* for his performance, as were Alexander as Oglow, Mrs. West as Zorilda, and Julia Drake as Selima, "whose beauty and merit were transcendently great upon this occasion." In his autobiography Joe Jefferson makes an interesting comment on *Timour the Tartar*:

> Of all theatrical entertainments, the equestrian drama is perhaps the most absurd. The actor and the horse refuse to unite; there is nothing of the centaur about them. I have seen the tyrant *Timour the Tartar* stride about the stage

78 *Gazette*, 3, 10 September 1819.

tempestuously, inspiring the audience with the idea that nothing could daunt the imperious spirit within him, but as soon as he espied the prancing steed that was to bear him to victory his passion cooled and with a lamb-like submission he would allow himself to be boosted up into the saddle, where he would sit unsteadily, looking the picture of misery.[79]

Despite Jefferson's opinion, *Timour the Tartar* was a popular spectacle. Drake performed it again in Frankfort on December 30, 1819, following the Lexington engagement. *Timour the Tartar* and *The Heir At Law*, advertised in the December 30 *Commentator*, were the only two plays announced in Frankfort in 1819.

Taxes levied by city officials on stage productions placed an extra financial burden on Drake and other western managers, who often had difficulty meeting their regular expenses. As early as 1811, the Lexington Trustees required all performers to pay up to thirty dollars per week, according to the price of admission.[80] Drake may have been forced to offer only a limited season in Frankfort in 1819 as a result of the forty-dollar-a-week tax demanded by the Frankfort Trustees. A critic of the tax argued in the *Commentator*, January 29, 1819, that Drake had been solicited to make the theatre in Frankfort respectable and that he had accomplished this at considerable expense and labor. The Trustees agreed to change the law, allowing Drake to contribute the receipts of one night's performance for "the benefit of the town." A number of newspaper notices indicate Drake's generosity with his charity benefits. During the same Frankfort engagement of 1819-1820 the *Commentator* announced on February 17, 1820, that his contribution to the relief of the inhabitants of Savannah amounted to $200.50. Johnston states that Drake seldom paid taxes as such for his Louisville Theatre but instead performed benefits for hospitals, churches, and charities.[81] On May 14, 1923, along with its

---

[79] Jefferson, *Autobiography*, p. 125.
[80] "Lexington Minute Book, 1782–1811" (manuscript, Kentucky Historical Society, Frankfort), p. 323.
[81] *History of Louisville*, 2: 64, quoted in *Courier-Journal*, 25 December 1921.

notice of *Macbeth*, the *Louisville Public Advertiser* stated that the receipts of May 21 would go to the trustees "to be applied for the fund appropriated by law for Draining the Ponds of Louisville."

Drama was not the only cultural activity sponsored by Drake in his circuit. He also made it possible for music lovers to hear musical concerts conducted by Anthony Philip Heinrich, a Bohemian musician who became "America's first composer."[82] Heinrich, like Drake, had wandered over the mountains and floated down the rivers to Kentucky, where he renewed his acquaintance with the Drake family in Lexington during the 1817 season. There on Wednesday, November 12, 1817, Heinrich, "assisted by the Principal Professors and Amateurs," performed a grand concert at Keene and Lamphear's Assembly Room. The program included Beethoven's *Sinfonia con Minuetto*; it was the first performance of a Beethoven symphony in America.[83] Aided by Samuel Drake, Jr., Alexander Drake, Francis Blisset, and some amateur musicians, Heinrich presented a two-part program of classical and light music. He was not only the first musician to introduce classical music into the West; he was also the first composer to use native "Indian themes and to display nationalistic American tendencies."[84] Heinrich and Drake collaborated again in Frankfort during the 1818 engagement and at the Louisville Theatre on June 8, 1819. Before his concert in Louisville Heinrich had gone into seclusion in a log house near Bardstown, Kentucky, but in January 1819 he moved to Jefferson County near Louisville. At the first Louisville concert he presented over twenty musical compositions and a between-the-parts recitation by Jones of Dryden's "celebrated Ode on St. Cecilia's day, or Alexander's Feast."[85] On January 26, 1820, the *Louisville Public Advertiser* announced the publication and performance of Heinrich's first musical work, *The Dawning of Music in Kentucky, or The Pleasures*

[82] Ibid., 21 October 1951.
[83] William Treat Upton, *Antony Philip Heinrich* (New York, 1939), introduction.
[84] *Courier-Journal*, 21 October 1951.
[85] Antony Philip Heinrich, "Scrapbook" (manuscript, Library of Congress).

of Harmony in Solitude. The review of the concert mentioned that Heinrich, appearing for the second time that season, gave a "specimen of his wonderful performance on the violin, executing amongst other pieces, his Variations to the tune of Yankee Doodle, in a style of excellence peculiarly his own." Both Alexander Drake and Samuel Drake, Jr., played the violin with "great éclat, assisted by Mr. Penner, on the grand piano forte, Mr. McClary on the violincello and Mr. —— on the flute."[86] Heinrich left Kentucky for Boston in 1823.[87]

It is difficult to imagine the production problems that faced Drake in Kentucky and in other areas during his first few years in the West. Transportation to and from the theatres in the circuit and outside the state presented an almost insurmountable problem, especially in bad weather. The difficult task of producing plays in drafty, dirty, makeshift buildings called "theatres" was matched only by the perennial chore of recruiting trained, responsible actors. As late as 1828, a traveler visiting the Louisville Theatre during a performance by Mrs. Alexander Drake reported that the house was almost filled, since Mrs. Drake was a favorite, but that the supporting company was very "ordinary." The players were costumed poorly and had not learned their lines properly. Not only did they play in a "vulgar style," but one performer was so intoxicated that "he was hardly able to keep his legs."[88] But Drake was determined to succeed. He rebuilt and redecorated theatres, sent troupes into rural areas, sponsored musical concerts and charity benefits, and gave the western audiences a variety of popular and classical drama.

After 1817 Drake faced the competition of other companies in Kentucky and surrounding areas, but the record shows that most of these troupes fared badly in comparison to the organized engagements managed by Drake. Turner's company in Cincinnati was described as a poor one, inadequately supported. Ludlow's troupe in Louisville and Cincinnati was wretched in

[86] *Louisville Public Advertisers,* 12 June 1819 (Weisert's unpublished notes).
[87] *Courier-Journal,* 21 October 1951.
[88] Bernhard, *Travels through North America,* p. 133.

comparison to Drake's regular performers. In 1817 John Palmer, a traveler, witnessed a strolling troupe's performance in Limestone, Kentucky; he recalled that they were a band from England who had given out handbills announcing their production of *The Honeymoon,* to be followed by an entertainment called *'Tis All a Farce.* Not only were the scenery and acting brought forth in a miserable manner, said Palmer, but he had to pay a dollar to witness the production. He thought, however, that the orchestra of Negroes, who performed tunes with two fiddles and two triangles, kept the audience in good humor.[89]

Difficult transportation kept the great stage stars of the East from visiting the western theatres during the early period of Drake's management. In later years, however, Drake entertained such celebrated actors as Junius Brutus Booth, the father of Edwin and John Wilkes Booth. Junius Booth became a close friend of the Drake family and often visited Drake's farm in Oldham County during his Louisville engagements. Johnston says that Drake was a fine fencer: "the audience was never so much pleased as in a combat with swords between him and the elder Booth."[90] America's first great tragedian, Edwin Forrest, while learning the acting profession, performed in Drake's Louisville Theatre in 1823 before moving to Cincinnati and Lexington. While in Cincinnati Forrest gave his first performances of Othello and many other roles, "with scarcely any knowledge of the text."[91] He returned to Drake's theatre as a star in 1839 to play Spartacus in *The Gladiator,* one of his most popular roles.

Another rising young actor, Thomas D. Rice, a comedian, appeared on the Drake stage in Louisville in 1828. He was a tall, "scrambling" looking man who was extremely modest and who always wore a strange hat "pointed down before and behind." Once while Rice was performing, he happened to glance out the rear stage door facing a yard and livery stable owned by a

---

[89] John Palmer, *Journal of Travels in the United States of North America and in Lower Canada . . .* (London, 1818), pp. 67-68.
[90] *History of Louisville,* 2: 329.
[91] *Theatrical Management,* p. 50.

man named Crow, or Crowe. There he saw an elderly, crippled Negro rubbing down horses and singing an improvised tune containing the words "Jump Jim Crow." The Negro added a comic dancing jump, or "hitch," at the end of each verse:

> Wheel about, turn about
>   Do jis so,
> And ebery time I wheel about
>   I jump Jim Crow[92]

It happened that Drake was producing at this time a Kentucky play called *The Rifle*. Rice, cast as a "Kentucky Cornfield Negro," used the song and dance of "Jump Jim Crow." The audience went wild with delight and called him back to the stage for many encores. Using the same mannerisms and adding several verses, Rice took the character to the eastern theatres, where he was an immediate success and where he acquired the name "Jim Crow" Rice. His song became a national popular tune. Only later did the name "Jim Crow" became associated with local segregation laws. The great American comedian Joe Jefferson made his debut on the stage with Rice at the age of four as "little Jim Crow." He dressed exactly like Rice and had copied to perfection the comedian's movements.[93]

Samuel Drake, Sr., outlived all his children and retired to his farm near Prospect, Kentucky, in Oldham County, overlooking the Ohio River. The family home, 150 acres of beautiful rolling land originally known as the "Barbour Grant," was located directly opposite Diamond Island. Drake died on his farm on October 18, 1854, at the age of 86. On October 19 the *Louisville Daily Journal*, after giving a brief biography, quoted Shakespeare's well-known line from *Macbeth*, "After life's fitful fever, he sleeps well."

The Drake name was associated with western stage production from 1815 to the period of Mrs. Alexander Drake's man-

---

[92] Laurence Hutton, *Curiosities of the American Stage* (New York, 1891), p. 117.
[93] Ibid.

agement after the old Louisville Theatre burned in 1843, a long and significant theatrical contribution by one family. But the theatrical trail had been broken many years before by John Vos, James Douglas, William Turner, and all the other actors who came across the mountains to bring the theatre to the West.

Bibliography

Acts Passed at the First Session of the Thirty-second General Assembly for the Commonwealth of Kentucky. Frankfort, Ky., 1824.

Adams, W. Davenport. *A Dictionary of the Drama: A Guide to the Plays, Players, and Playhouses of the United Kingdom and America, from the Earliest Times to the Present.* Vol. I: A-G (no other volumes published). Philadelphia: J. B. Lippincott, 1905.

American Republic. Frankfort, Ky.

Argus of Western America. Frankfort, Ky.

Barrickman, W. C. "Early Days in Kentucky and Elsewhere," *The Oldham Era,* 1 March, 1940.

Bernard, John. *Retrospections of America, 1797–1811.* New York: Harper and Bros., 1887.

Bernhard, Duke of Saxe-Weimar Eisenach. *Travels through North America, during the Years 1825 and 1826.* 2 vols. Philadelphia: Carey, Lea, and Carey, 1828.

Brown, Orlando. "The Governors of Kentucky [1792–1824]." *Register of the Kentucky Historical Society* 49 (April 1951): 93-112.

Brown, T. Alliston. *A History of the New York Stage from the First Performance in 1732 to 1901.* 3 vols. New York: Dick and Fitzgerald, 1870.

Carson, William G. B. *The Theatre on the Frontier: The Early Years of the St. Louis Stage.* Chicago: University of Chicago Press, 1932.

Clapp, William W., Jr. *A Record of the Boston Stage.* Boston: James Munroe, 1853.

Coad, Oral Sumner, and Mims, Edwin, Jr. *The Pageant of America.* 15 vols. New Haven, Conn.: Yale University Press, 1929.

Coleman, J. Winston, Jr. *Stage-Coach Days in the Bluegrass*. Louisville, Ky.: Standard Press, 1935.

————. *The Court-Houses of Lexington (Fayette County, Kentucky)*. Lexington: privately printed, 1937.

Collins, Lewis. *History of Kentucky*. 2 vols. Covington, Ky.: Collins, 1882.

Commentator. Frankfort, Ky.

Courier-Journal. Louisville, Ky.

Cowell, Joe. *Thirty Years Passed among the Players in England and America*. New York: Harper and Bros., 1884.

Crum, Mable Tyree. "The History of the Lexington Theatre from the Beginning to 1860." 2 vols. Ph.D. dissertation, University of Kentucky, 1956.

Cuming, Fortescue. *Sketches of a Tour to the Western Country, through the States of Ohio and Kentucky*. . . . Vol. 4, *Early Western Travels, 1748–1846*. . . ., ed. Reuben Gold Thwaites. Cleveland: Arthur H. Clark, 1904.

Daily Focus. Louisville, Ky.

Dunlap, William. *The History of the American Theatre*. New York: J. J. Harper, 1832.

Fayette County Court Deed Book B. Lexington, Ky.

Fayette County Court Deed Book C. Lexington, Ky.

Fayette County Court Deed Book S. Lexington, Ky.

Ford, George D. *These Were Actors: A Story of the Chapmans and the Drakes*. New York: Library Publishers, 1955.

Fordham, Elias Pym. *Personal Narratives of Travel in Virginia, Maryland, Pennsylvania, Ohio, Indiana, Kentucky*; . . . Cleveland: Arthur H. Clark, 1906.

Franklin County Deed Book 1. Frankfort, Ky.

Franklin County Deed Book 2. Frankfort, Ky.

Gilbert, Anne Hartley. *The Stage Reminiscences of Mrs. Gilbert*. New York: Charles Scribner and Sons, 1901.

Hardin, Bayliss E. "Notes from Frankfort Newspapers." Manuscript, Kentucky Historical Society, Frankfort.

Hartnoll, Phyllis. *The Oxford Companion to the Theatre*. London: Oxford University Press, 1951.

Heinrich, Anthony Philip. "Scrapbook." Manuscript, Library of Congress.

Hewitt, Bernard. *Theatre, U.S.A.: 1668 to 1957*. New York: McGraw-Hill, 1959.

Hill, West T., Jr. "A Study of the Macauley's Theatre in Louisville, Kentucky, 1873–1880." Ph.D. dissertation, University of Iowa, 1954.

Hornblow, Arthur. *A History of the Theatre in America.* 2 vols. New York: Lippincott, 1919.

Hutton, Laurence. *Curiosities of the American Stage.* New York: Harper and Bros., 1891.

Ireland, Joseph N. *Record of the New York Stage from 1750 to 1860.* 2 vols. New York: T. H. Morrell, 1866.

Jefferson County Deed Book 8. Louisville, Ky.

Jefferson County Deed Book K. Louisville, Ky.

Jefferson, Joseph. *The Autobiography of Joseph Jefferson.* New York: The Century Co., 1889–1890.

Johnson, Allen, ed. *Dictionary of American Biography.* 22 vols. New York: Charles Scribner's Sons, 1928–1958.

Johnson, L. F. *The History of Franklin County, Kentucky.* Frankfort, Ky.: Roberts Printing Co., 1912.

Johnston, J. Stoddard. *Memorial History of Louisville from Its First Settlement to the Year 1896.* 2 vols. Chicago: American Biographical Publishing Co., 1895.

Kentucky Gazette. Lexington, Ky.

Langworthy, Helen. "The Theatre in the Lower Valley of the Ohio, 1797-1860." Ph.D. dissertation, State University of Iowa, 1926.

Lee, Alfred McClung. "Trends in Commercial Entertainment in Pittsburgh As Reflected in the Advertising in Pittsburgh's Newspapers (1790–1860)." Master's thesis, University of Pittsburgh, 1931.

"Lexington Minute Book, 1782–1811." Manuscript, Kentucky Historical Society, Frankfort.

Lexington Reporter.

Louisville Correspondent.

Louisville Directory for the Year 1832. Louisville, Ky.: Richard W. Otis, 1832.

Louisville Daily Journal.

Louisville Public Advertiser.

Ludlow, Noah Miller. *Dramatic Life As I Found It.* New York: Benjamin Blom, 1966.

McMurtrie, Henrico. *Sketches of Louisville and Its Environs.* Louisville, Ky.: S. Penn, 1819.

Mason County Court Order Book F. Washington, Ky.

168   BIBLIOGRAPHY

Meek, Beryl. "A Record of the Theatre in Lexington, Kentucky, 1790–1850." Master's thesis, State University of Iowa, 1930.

Melish, John. *Travels in the United States of America in the Years 1806, 1807, and 1809, 1810, and 1811.* 2 vols. Philadelphia: Thomas and George Palmer, 1812.

Morris, Clara. *Life on the Stage.* New York: McClure, Phillips, 1902.

Nicoll, Allardyce. *A History of the English Drama, 1661–1900.* 6 vols. Cambridge: Cambridge University Press, 1959.

————. *The Development of the Theatre: A Study of Theatrical Art from the Beginning to the Present Day.* London: George G. Harrap, 1958.

Odell, George C. D. *Annals of the New York Stage.* 15 vols. New York: Columbia University Press, 1927–1949.

Palladium. Frankfort, Ky.

Palmer, John. *Journal of Travels in the United States of North America and in Lower Canada (Performed in the Year) 1817.* London: R. and R. Gilbert, 1818.

Perrin, W. H., Battle, J. H., and Kniffen, G. C. *Kentucky: A History of the State.* Louisville, Ky.: F. A. Battery, 1887.

Peter, Robert. *History of Fayette County, Kentucky, with an Outline Sketch of the Blue Grass Region.* Chicago: O. L. Baskind, 1802.

Phelps, Henry Pitts. *Players of a Century: A Record of the Albany Stage.* Albany, N.Y.: Joseph McDonaugh, 1880.

Quinn, Arthur Hobson. *A History of the American Drama from the Beginning to the Civil War.* New York: F. S. Crofts, 1946.

————. *Edgar Allan Poe: A Critical Biography.* New York: D. Appleton-Century, 1941.

Ranck, George W. *History of Lexington, Kentucky, Its Early Annals and Recent Progress.* Cincinnati, Ohio: R. Clarke, 1872.

"Record of the Proceedings of the Board of Trustees of Transylvania University: 1799–1810." Manuscript, Transylvania University Library, Lexington, Ky.

Rowell, George. *The Victorian Theatre: A Survey.* New York: Oxford University Press, 1956.

Rusk, Ralph Leslie. *The Literature of the Middle Western Frontier.* 2 vols. New York: Columbia University Press, 1925.

Seilhamer, G. C. *The History of the American Theatre.* 3 vols. Philadelphia: Glove Printing House, 1891.

Smith, Solomon F. *Theatrical Management in the West and South for Thirty Years.* New York: Harper and Bros., 1868.

Smither, Nellie. *A History of the English Theatre in New Orleans.* New York: Benjamin Blom, 1967.

Staples, Charles. *History of Pioneer Lexington.* Lexington, Ky.: Transylvania Press, 1939.

––––––. "The Amusements and Diversions of Early Lexington." Manuscript, Lexington Public Library, 1925.

Stephen, Leslie, and Lee, Sidney, eds. *Dictionary of National Biography.* 24 vols. London: Oxford University Press, 1917.

Stewart's Kentucky Herald. Lexington, Ky.

" 'The Poor Soldier'—A Revival of an Old Comic Opera to Be Staged in Cincinnati." *Bulletin of the Historical and Philosophical Society of Ohio* 9 (July 1951): 234-37.

The Times. London.

Trollope, Frances. *Domestic Manners of the Americans.* Edited by Donald Smalley. New York: Alfred A. Knopf, 1949.

Upton, William Treat. *Anthony Philip Heinrich.* New York: Columbia University Press, 1939.

Venable, W. H. *Literary Culture in the Ohio Valley.* Cincinnati, Ohio: R. Clarke, 1891.

Washington Mirror. Washington, Ky.

Weisert, John J. "Beginnings of the Kentucky Theatre Circuit." *Filson Club History Quarterly* 34 (July 1960): 264-85.

––––––. "The First Decade of Sam Drake's Louisville Theatre." *Filson Club History Quarterly* 39 (October 1965): 287-310.

––––––. Unpublished notes from Frankfort newspapers.

Wemyss, Francis C. *Chronology of the American Stage from 1752 to 1852.* New York: W. Taylor, 1852.

Western Citizen. Paris, Ky.

Western Courier. Louisville, Ky.

Western Spy. Cincinnati, Ohio.

Western World. Frankfort, Ky.

Appendix

Record of Performances, 1790-1820

THIS appendix lists in chronological order only dramatic performances announced by newspapers in Kentucky towns and in Cincinnati during the period from 1790 to 1820. Included are the first titles of the plays, the dramatists (when known), the days and dates of performance, and the theatre or other place of performance (when known). Authors' names are given only with the first listing of each play.

The following table lists the ten most popular playwrights during the early period:

Playwright	No. of Performances	No. of Plays	Single Performance Record
COLMAN, the younger	65	16	*The Mountaineers* 8
SHAKESPEARE	38	8	*Macbeth* 9
SHERIDAN, R. B.	29	4	*Pizarro* 19
O'KEEFFE	26	9	*The Poor Soldier* 11
MORTON	26	8	*Children in the Wood* 7
BICKERSTAFFE	21	4	*The Spoiled Child* 7
KENNY	20	5	*Raising the Wind* 6
DUNLAP	19	6	*The Stranger* 9
INCHBALD	19	5	*The Midnight Hour* 8
CUMBERLAND	15	5	*The Jew* 8

A statistical summary of western stage production during the early period reveals some interesting facts. The western newspapers in the theatrical centers recorded 614 performances of serious dramas, comedies, farces, musical plays, interludes, and pantomimes. Kentucky, with three drama-producing towns, recorded 560, or roughly 90 percent of the total number of western performances. These 614 performances represented 193 theatrical offerings by

80 dramatists. George Colman, the younger, by far the most popular playwright, had 65 performances of 16 plays. His *The Mountaineers*, with 8 showings, was the favorite, followed by *The Poor Gentleman*, with 7. Shakespeare was second to Colman in popularity with 38 productions of 8 plays; *Macbeth*, with 9 performances, appears to have been the favorite. Richard Brinsley Sheridan's adaptation *Pizarro*, with 19 performances, had nearly twice as many showings as any other play.

1790

LEXINGTON (*Transylvania University*)

Unnamed tragedy and farce		Fri., April 10

1797

WASHINGTON COURTHOUSE

Douglas	John Home	Thurs., Oct. 12
Love-a-la-Mode	Charles Macklin	
The Padlock	Isaac Bickerstaffe	

1799

LEXINGTON COURTHOUSE

The Busy Body	Susannah Centlivre	Fri., March 1
Love-a-la-Mode		
He Would Be a Soldier	Frederick Pilon	Tues., March 5
All the World's a Stage	Isaac Jackman	
The West Indian	Richard Cumberland	Thurs., Nov. 29
The Citizen	Arthur Murphy	

1801

LEXINGTON (*unlocated theatre*)

The School for Arrogance	Thomas Holcroft	Thurs., May 21
The Farmer	John O'Keeffe	

CINCINNATI (*unlocated theatre*)

The Poor Soldier	O'Keeffe	Thurs., Oct. 1

1802

LEXINGTON (*unlocated theatre*)

The Gamester	Edward Moore	Thurs., Jan. 14
The Dead Alive	O'Keeffe	

CINCINNATI (*unlocated theatre*)

The Poor Soldier	Wed., Feb. 19

1806

CINCINNATI THEATRE (*Front Street*)

Secrets Worth Knowing	Thomas Morton	Tues., Sept. 30
Love-a-la-Mode		

BRYAN'S STATION SCHOOL (*near Lexington*)

She Stoops to Conquer	Oliver Goldsmith	Mon., Oct. 6

CINCINNATI THEATRE (*Front Street*)

The Mountaineers	George Colman, the younger	Thurs., Dec. 5
The Padlock		

1807

LEXINGTON (*Traveller's Hall*)

The Poor Gentleman	Colman	Thurs., March 12

FRANKFORT (*unlocated theatre*)

The Brave Irishman	Thomas Sheridan	Thurs., Dec. 17
The Padlock		

1808

LEXINGTON (*Traveller's Hall*)

Speed the Plough	Morton	Wed., Jan. 6
The Review	Colman	

LEXINGTON THEATRE

The Sailor's Daughter	Cumberland	Wed., Oct. 12
Ways and Means	Colman	

LEXINGTON THEATRE

The Sailor's Daughter		Sat., Oct. 15
Ways and Means		
Lovers' Vows	Elizabeth Inchbald	Wed., Oct. 19
Speed the Plough		Sat., Nov. 5
Speed the Plough		Wed., Nov. 9
The Devil to Pay	Charles Coffey	
The Castle Spectre	M. G. Lewis	Fri., Dec. 14

1809

LEXINGTON THEATRE

Animal Magnetism	Inchbald	Sat., April 15
No Song, No Supper	Prince Hoare	
The Jew	Cumberland	Mon., April 24
Sylvester Daggerwood	Colman	
Tell Truth and Shame the Devil	William Dunlap	Mon., May 8
The Irishman in London	William Macready	
Douglas		Sat., Aug. 5
Columbus	Morton	Sat., Sept. 23
The Man of Enterprize	Charles Shillito	
Columbus		Sat., Sept. 30
Children in the Wood	Morton	

FRANKFORT (*Mrs. Love's House*)

The Heir at Law	Colman	Thurs., Oct. 5
Honest Thieves	Thomas Knight	

LEXINGTON THEATRE

Columbus		Sat., Oct. 7
Children in the Wood		
Speed the Plough		Sat., Oct. 28
Children in the Wood		

FRANKFORT (*Mrs. Love's House*)

The Way to Get Married	Morton	Mon., Oct. 30
The Sixty-Third Letter	W. C. Oulton	

1810

LEXINGTON THEATRE

The Busy Body		Wed., March 14
The Sixty-Third Letter		
The Busy Body		Sat., March 17
The Sixty-Third Letter		
Blue Beard	Colman	Sat., April 21
The Devil to Pay		
Revenge	Edward Young	Mon., May 7
The Village Lawyer	Macready	
Revenge		Sat., May 12
A House to Be Sold	James Cobb	
The Rivals	Richard Brinsley Sheridan	Wed., June 6
A House to Be Sold		
Abaellino	Dunlap	Sat., July 7
The Padlock		
Abaellino		Sat., July 14
Children in the Wood		
The Heir at Law		Sat., Aug. 18
The Prisoner at Large	O'Keeffe	
Pizarro	R. B. Sheridan	Sat., Sept. 15
Honest Thieves		
Pizarro		Thurs., Sept. 20
Honest Thieves		
Pizarro		Sat., Sept. 22
High Life below Stairs	James Townley	
Pizarro		Wed., Sept. 26
High Life below Stairs		
The Castle Spectre		Thurs., Oct. 4
Jonathan Postfree	L. Beach	
Macbeth	William Shakespeare	Thurs., Oct. 11
Raising the Wind	James Kenny	
Macbeth		Wed., Oct. 17
Raising the Wind		
The Child of Nature	Inchbald	Sat., Dec. 22
Sprigs of Laurel	O'Keeffe	
Reconciliation	A. F. von Kotzebue	Wed., Dec. 26
The Weathercock	John T. Allingham	

1811

FRANKFORT (*Price's Inn*)

Lovers' Vows		Sat., Jan. 12
The Weathercock		
The Gamester		Mon., Jan. 21
The Waterman	Charles Dibdin	

LEXINGTON THEATRE

Lovers' Vows		Sat., Jan. 26
Love-a-la-Mode		
Lovers' Vows		Wed., Jan. 30
Love-a-la-Mode		
Isabella	Thomas Southerne	Sat., Feb. 9
The Spoiled Child	Bickerstaffe	
The Midnight Hour	Inchbald	Wed., Feb. 13
Fortune's Frolic	Allingham	
Romeo and Juliet	Shakespeare	Sat., Feb. 23
Harlequin's Vagaries (pantomime)		
The Midnight Hour		Wed., Feb. 27
The Village Lawyer		
The Curfew	John Tobin	Sat., March 2
The Prize	Hoare	
Secrets Worth Knowing		Wed., March 6
Catherine and Petruchio	David Garrick	
A Tale of Mystery	Holcroft	Sat., March 9
The Farm House	Charles Kemble	
Othello	Shakespeare	Wed., March 13
Love Laughs at Locksmiths	Colman	
The Robbers	Friedrich Schiller	Sat., March 16
The Spoiled Child		
Barbarossa	John Browne	Wed., March 20
Love and Magic (pantomime)		
Othello		Sat., March 23
Love Laughs at Locksmiths		
Abaellino		Sat., April 6
The Mock Doctor	Henry Fielding	
The Soldier's Daughter	Andrew Cherry	Sat., April 13
All the World's A Stage		
Adelmorn, the Outlaw	Lewis	Sat., April 20

A *Budget of Blunders*   C. Kemble
The Roman Father   William Whitehead   Sat., April 27
The Jew and the Doctor Thomas Dibdin
The Gamester   Sat., May 4
The Weathercock

CINCINNATI THEATRE (*near Columbian Inn*)

Animal Magnetism   Mon., May 27
The Review
Douglas   Mon., June 3
The Romp   Bickerstaffe

LEXINGTON THEATRE

King Henry IV   Shakespeare   Sat., June 8
Matrimony   Kenny

CINCINNATI THEATRE (*near Columbian Inn*)

Secrets Worth Knowing   Mon., June 10
The Poor Soldier
The Birthday   T. Dibdin   Mon., June 17
The Weathercock
The Clown's Vagaries (pantomime)
Douglas   Mon., June 24
The Padlock

LEXINGTON THEATRE

Tekeli   Theodore Hook   Sat., June 29
Matrimony
Tekeli   Thurs., July 4
The Father Outwitted Lope de Vega
Point of Honor   C. Kemble   Sat., Aug. 3
Love-a-la-Mode
The Poor Gentleman   Colman   Sat., Sept. 21
The Irishman in Naples (author unknown)
Venice Preserved   Thomas Otway   Sat., Sept. 28
The Mock Doctor
Adelmorn, the Outlaw   Wed., Oct. 2
The Ghost   Centlivre
Who Wants a Guinea?   Colman   Sat., Oct. 5
Raising the Wind

LEXINGTON THEATRE

Douglas		Sat., Oct. 12
Yes or No	Isaac Pocock	
Mahomet, the Imposter	James Miller	Sat., Oct. 19
The Review		
The Will for the Deed	T. Dibdin	Sat., Oct. 26
The Poor Soldier		
The Heir at Law		Sat., Nov. 2
The Poor Soldier		
Wild Oats	O'Keeffe	Sat., Nov. 23
Three Weeks after Marriage	Murphy	
The Stranger	Dunlap	Wed., Nov. 27
The Mock Doctor		
The Wheel of Fortune	Cumberland	Sat., Nov. 30
High Life below Stairs		

1811–1812

FRANKFORT THEATRE

Hamlet	Shakespeare	Mon., Dec. 9
Three Weeks after Marriage		
The Road to Ruin	Holcroft	Wed., Dec. 11
Matrimony		
Point of Honor		Fri., Dec. 13
High Life below Stairs		
The Mountaineers	Colman	Wed., Dec. 18
The Village Lawyer		
Venice Preserved		Fri., Dec. 27
Love-a-la-Mode		
Catherine and Petruchio		Wed., Jan. 1
The Ghost		

1812

LEXINGTON (*Traveller's Hall*)

The Mountaineers	Wed., Jan. 1
High Life below Stairs	

LEXINGTON (*Hotel Theatre*)

Macbeth	Sat., Jan. 4
Sprigs of Laurel	

FRANKFORT THEATRE

Pizarro		Fri., Jan. 10
Love-a-la-Mode		
Venice Preserved		Wed., Jan. 15
Catherine and Petruchio		
Tekeli		Thurs., Jan. 16
Sprigs of Laurel		

LEXINGTON THEATRE

Pizarro		Sat., Jan. 18

FRANKFORT THEATRE

Pizarro		Mon., Jan. 20
Blue Devils	Colman	
Macbeth		Wed., Jan. 29
Blue Devils		
Tekeli		Mon., Jan. 27
Sprigs of Laurel		
The Stranger		Fri., Feb. 7
The Romp		
The Stranger		Thurs., Feb. 13
The Spoiled Child		

LEXINGTON THEATRE

Othello		Tues., Feb. 18
Blue Devils		
The Battle of Hexam	Colman	Mon., Feb. 24
The Maid of the Oaks	John Burgoyne	
Pizarro		Wed., Feb. 26
The Review		
Pizarro		Wed., March 11
The Review		
Pizarro		Wed., March 18
Blue Devils		
The Curfew	Tobin	Sat., March 21
Three Weeks after Marriage		
The Death of André	Dunlap	Wed., March 25
The Romp		
Isabella		Sat., March 28
The Poor Soldier		
Rudolphe	John Turnbull	Sat., April 4

LEXINGTON THEATRE

The Romp		
The Soldier's Daughter		Thurs., April 9
The Prisoner at Large		
De Montfort	Joanne Baille	Wed., April 15
The Village Lawyer		
Zara	Aaron Hill	Sat., April 25
Children in the Wood		
John Bull	Colman	Sat., May 30
The Sixty-Third Letter		
The Blind Bargain	Frederick Reynolds	Thurs., June 11
The Spoiled Child		
Point of Honor		Sat., Aug. 1
The Midnight Hour		

FRANKFORT THEATRE

She Stoops to Conquer		Wed., Aug. 19
Two Strings to		
Your Bow	Robert Jephson	

LEXINGTON THEATRE

The Jew		Thurs., Oct. 1
The Purse	J. D. Cross	
The Rival Queens	Nathaniel Lee	Wed., Oct. 7
Animal Magnetism		
The Mountaineers		Sat., Oct. 10
Who's the Dupe?	Hannah Cowley	
Blue Beard		Tues., Oct. 13
The Adopted Child	Samuel Birch	
The Doubtful Son	William Dimond	Wed., Nov. 4
The Poor Soldier		
The Rivals		Wed., Nov. 25
The Padlock		
The Merchant of Venice	Shakespeare	Sat., Nov. 28
The Irishman in London	Macready	
Inkle and Yarico	Colman	Tues., Dec. 1
The Bee Hive	John Millingen	
The Waterman		
The Honeymoon	Tobin	Sat., Dec. 5
The Faithful Irishman	(author unknown)	

1812–1813

FRANKFORT THEATRE

The Honeymoon		Wed., Dec. 9
The Village Lawyer		
The Rivals		Wed., Dec. 16
Sprigs of Laurel		
Pizarro		Wed., Jan. 20
Miss in Her Teens	Garrick	
Blue Beard		Thurs., Jan. 28
The Romp		

1813

LOUISVILLE THEATRE

Pizarro		Fri., March 26
Raising the Wind		

CINCINNATI THEATRE

The Execution	Douglas Jerrold	Tues., March 30
The Battle of		
Tippecanoe	(author unknown)	

LEXINGTON THEATRE

The Foundling of the		
Forest	Dimond	Wed., May 19
The Virgin of the Sun	Dunlap	Wed., May 26
The Padlock		
The Mountaineers		Wed., June 2
Miss in Her Teens		
The Busy Body		Wed., June 9
Sylvester Daggerwood		
Man and Wife	Samuel Arnold	Wed., June 16
Sprigs of Laurel		
The Road to Ruin		Wed., June 23
The Purse		
The Soldier's Benefit	(author unknown)	Tues., June 29
Who's the Dupe?		
Jane Shore	Nicholas Rowe	Sat., July 3
The Spoiled Child		

CINCINNATI THEATRE

Naval Representation		Sat., July 3
Yankee Chronology	Dunlap	

LEXINGTON THEATRE

Romeo and Juliet	Shakespeare	Sat., July 17
Highland Reel	O'Keeffe	
Revenge		Sat., July 24
Ella Rosenberg	Kenny	
The Stranger		Sat., July 31
The Day after the Wedding	Marie Kemble	
Abaellino		Sat., Aug. 7
St. Patrick's Day	R. B. Sheridan	
The Stranger		Sat., Aug. 14
How to Die for Love	Kotzebue	
The Carmelite	Cumberland	Sat., Aug. 21
Ella Rosenberg		
Bunker Hill	John D. Burk	Thurs., Aug. 26
How to Die for Love		
The Man of Fortitude	Dunlap	Sat., Sept. 4
St. Patrick's Day		
Fontainville Forest	James Boaden	Wed., Oct. 6
Blue Devils		
Tit for Tat	Joseph Atkinson	Sat., Oct. 16
The Widow of Malabar	Mariana Starke	Sat., Oct. 23
The Widow of Malabar		Sat., Oct. 30
The Widow of Malabar		Sat., Nov. 6
The Spanish Barber	Colman	Sat., Nov. 13
Don Juan (pantomime)	Carlo Delpini	

1814

LOUISVILLE THEATRE

Jane Shore		Wed., Feb. 16
The Sleepwalker	Oulton	
The Voice of Nature	Dunlap	Wed., Feb. 23
St. Patrick's Day		
Tit for Tat		Wed., March 2
Twenty Years Ago	Pocock	

The Jew		Wed., March 9
The Adopted Child		
The Merchant of Venice		Wed., March 16
How to Die for Love		
Fontainville Forest		Wed., March 23
Catherine and Petruchio		
Hamlet		Wed., March 30
Tell Truth and Shame the Devil		
Revenge		Wed., April 6
The Day after the Wedding		
The Wanderer	Kotzebue	Wed., April 13
Modern Antiques	O'Keeffe	
Hamlet		Wed., April 20
The Purse		
Adelmorn, the Outlaw		Wed., April 27
Highland Reel		

LEXINGTON THEATRE

Reconciliation		Sat., May 28
The Sleepwalker		
Richard III	Shakespeare	Wed., June 1
The Purse		
The Stranger		Wed., June 8
Blue Devils		

LOUISVILLE THEATRE

The Mayor of Garratt	Samuel Foote	Mon., Aug. 29
Venice Preserved		

1815

LEXINGTON THEATRE

Who Wants a Guinea?		Mon., Jan. 16
The Boarding House	Samuel Beazley	

CINCINNATI THEATRE

The Stranger	Mon., April 3
Love Laughs at Locksmiths	
Man and Wife	Wed., April 12

CINCINNATI THEATRE

Of Age Tomorrow	T. Dibdin	
Richard III		Mon., April 17
All the World's a Stage		
The Heir at Law		Fri., May 5
Sylvester Daggerwood		
The Mayor of Garratt		
Macbeth		Wed., May 10
Pizarro		Fri., May 12
The Black Forest (pantomime)		Fri., Oct. 13

LEXINGTON THEATRE

The Doubtful Son		Wed., June 14
A Budget of Blunders	C. Kemble	
King Lear	Shakespeare	Mon., June 9
The Day after the Wedding		
Lovers' Vows		Mon., June 26
Darkness Visible	Hook	
The Wonder	Centlivre	Thurs., June 29
Yes or No		
The Wheel of Fortune		Mon., July 3
The Spoiled Child		
The Stranger		Mon., July 10
Children in the Wood		
The Castle Spectre		Mon., July 17
The Weathercock		
The Foundling of the Forest		Thurs., July 20
Hamlet		Mon., July 24
Raising the Wind		
The School of Reform	Morton	Thurs., July 27
A Cure for the Heart Ache	Morton	Mon., July 31
How to Die for Love		
The Citizen		
The Poor Gentleman		Mon., Aug. 7
The Poor Soldier		
She Stoops to Conquer		Thurs., Aug. 10
Highland Reel		
Town and Country, Which Is Best?	Morton	Tues., Aug. 15

Of Age Tomorrow		
Pizarro		Tues., Aug. 22
Rosina	Frances Brooke	
Othello		Thurs., Aug. 24
Gustavus Vasa	Henry Brooke	Tues., Aug. 29
The Devil to Pay		
Bunker Hill		Tues., Sept. 12
Blue Beard		
The Merchant of Venice		Tues., Sept. 19
Father Outwitted		
Town and Country, Which Is Best?		Thurs., Sept. 21
The Purse		
George Barnwell	George Lillo	Tues., Sept. 26
The Fortress	Hook	
Henry IV		Tues., Oct. 3
The Village Lawyer		
John Bull		Mon., Oct. 9
The Blind Boy	Kenny	

FRANKFORT THEATRE

The Mountaineers	Mon., Dec. 4
The Midnight Hour	
Speed the Plough	Mon., Dec. 11
Of Age Tomorrow	
The Merchant of Venice	Mon., Dec. 18
The Purse	

1816

CINCINNATI THEATRE

The Weathercock	Mon., Jan. 1
How to Die for Love	
Point of Honor	Tues., Jan. 9
How to Die for Love	

LOUISVILLE THEATRE

The Heir at Law	Wed., Feb. 28
The Midnight Hour	
Reconciliation	Wed., March 6

LOUISVILLE THEATRE

Robin Hood and		
Little John	(author unknown)	
Adelgitha	Lewis	Mon., March 11
The Lying Valet	Garrick	
The Jew		Wed., March 13
Honest Thieves		

CINCINNATI THEATRE

A Cure for the Heart Ache	Wed., March 20
Sylvester Daggerwood	

LOUISVILLE THEATRE

Man and Wife		Thurs., March 21
The Quaker	C. Dibdin	

CINCINNATI THEATRE

Raising the Wind	Fri., March 29
Jack in Distress (pantomime)	
The Romp	

LOUISVILLE THEATRE

The Blind Boy		Wed., April 3
The Poor Gentleman		
The Kiss	Stephen Clarke	Wed., April 3
The Blind Boy		

CINCINNATI THEATRE

A Cure for the Heart Ache	Fri., April 5
Love Laughs at Locksmiths	

LOUISVILLE THEATRE

John Bull		Fri., April 19
The Poor Soldier		
The Castle Spectre		Fri., April 26
Rosina		
Adrian and Orilla	Dimond	Fri., May 3
The Review		
She Stoops to Conquer		Fri., May 10
A Tale of Mystery	Holcroft	

The Merchant of Venice		Tues., May 14
A Tale of Mystery		

LEXINGTON THEATRE

The Foundling of the Forest		Tues., May 21
The Poor Soldier		
Adrian and Orilla		Tues., May 21
The Review		
Reconciliation		Mon., June 3
The Blind Boy		
Othello		Wed., June 5
The Purse		
She Stoops to Conquer		Mon., June 10
No Song, No Supper		
Inkle and Yarico		Mon., June 17
Love Laughs at Locksmiths		
Man and Wife		Mon., June 24
Animal Magnetism		
The Kiss		Mon., July 1
A Tale of Mystery		
Adrian and Orilla		Mon., Sept. 30
The Liar	Foote	
Macbeth		Tues., Oct. 8
The Jew and the Doctor		
Hamlet		Tues., Oct. 15
The Irishman in London		
Man and Wife		Tues., Oct. 22
Catherine and Petruchio		
Othello		Tues., Oct. 29
The Poor Soldier		
The Road to Ruin		Tues., Nov. 5
A Budget of Blunders		
The Poor Gentleman		Tues., Nov. 12
The Agreeable Surprise	O'Keeffe	
The Castle Spectre		Thurs., Nov. 14
Plot Counterplot	C. Kemble	
The Busy Body		Mon., Nov. 18
The Miller and His Men	Pocock	
The Mountaineers		Thurs., Nov. 20
Lock and Key	Hoare	

LEXINGTON THEATRE

The Jew	Tues., Nov. 26
Love Laughs at Locksmiths	

1817

CINCINNATI THEATRE

The Castle Spectre	Fri., Jan. 31
Of Age Tomorrow	
Pizarro	Fri., Feb. 21
Harlequin in the Moon (pantomime)	

LOUISVILLE THEATRE

The Liar	Mon., March 3

CINCINNATI THEATRE

The Merchant of Venice	Fri., March 14
Love Laughs at Locksmiths	

LOUISVILLE THEATRE

Pizarro		Mon., March 17
Who's the Dupe?		
Douglas		Sat., March 22
Turn Out	Kenny	
The Honeymoon		Thurs., April 10
The Liar		
The Way to Get Married		Thurs., April 17
The Midnight Hour		

CINCINNATI THEATRE

Barbarossa	Fri., July 11
Darkness Visible	

PARIS THEATRE

Turn Out	Fri., Aug. 15
Sylvester Daggerwood	
The Quaker	Sat., Aug. 23

LEXINGTON THEATRE

Speed the Plough		Thurs., Aug. 28
The Dramatist	Reynolds	Sat., Aug. 30

Who's the Dupe?		
Love in a Village	Bickerstaffe	
Past Ten O'clock, and		
a Rainy Night	(author unknown)	Sat., Sept. 6
Such Things Are	Inchbald	Sat., Sept. 13
The Padlock		
Americans in Algiers	Susannah Rowson	Sat., Sept. 20
Mr. H	Charles Lamb	

CINCINNATI THEATRE

Oroonoko	Southerne	Fri., Sept. 26

LEXINGTON THEATRE

Love in a Village		Thurs., Oct. 2
The Blind Boy		
The Castle Spectre		Sat., Oct. 4
The Quaker		
The Provoked Husband	Cibber-VanBrugh	Sat., Oct. 11
The Irishman in London		
The Jew		Sat., Oct. 18
The Forty Thieves	Colman	
The Forty Thieves		Thurs., Oct. 23
Macbeth		Sat., Oct. 25
'Tis All a Farce	Allingham	
Pizarro		
Catherine and Petruchio		Thurs., Oct. 30
He Would Be a Soldier		Sat., Nov. 1
Sylvester Daggerwood		
Three and the Deuce	Hoare	Sat., Nov. 8
The Miller and His Men		
The Merchant of Venice		Sat., Nov. 15
The Lying Valet		

CINCINNATI THEATRE

Bertram	Charles R. Maturin	Fri., Nov. 21

1818

LEXINGTON THEATRE

Macbeth		Fri., Sept. 4
The Weathercock		

LEXINGTON THEATRE

Pizarro		Wed., Sept. 9
Fortune's Frolic		
The Foundling of the Forest		Sat., Sept. 12
Tit for Tat		
The Iron Chest	Colman	Wed., Sept. 16
Catherine and Petruchio		
The Magpie and the Maid	Pocock	Wed., Sept. 23
The Midnight Hour		
The Magpie and the Maid		Sat., Sept. 26
The Hunter of the Alps	Dimond	
The Jew		Wed., Sept. 30
St. Patrick's Day		
The Honeymoon		Sat., Oct. 3
The Miller and His Men		
The Forty Thieves		Fri., Oct. 9
Reconciliation		
The Gamester		Wed., Oct. 14
The Turnpike Gate	Knight	
The Forty Thieves		Fri., Oct. 16
Reconciliation		
Isabella		Sat., Oct. 17
Ways and Means		
Alfonso, King of Castile	Lewis	Sat., Oct. 24
'Tis All a Farce		
Town and Country, Which Is Best?		Wed., Oct. 28
Children in the Wood		
The Voice of Nature		Sat., Oct. 31
Sylvester Daggerwood		
The Sleepwalker		
The School for Scandal	R. B. Sheridan	Wed., Nov. 4
The Old Maid	Murphy	
Henry IV		Sat., Nov. 7
Fortune's Frolic		
She Stoops to Conquer		Wed., Nov. 11
Lock and Key		
The Poor Gentleman		Sat., Nov. 14
Ella Rosenberg		
The Foundling of the Forest		Wed., Nov. 18
Sprigs of Laurel		

The Soldier's Daughter		Sat., Nov. 20
The Forty Thieves		

1819

LOUISVILLE THEATRE

Macbeth		Mon., March 3
The Old Maid		
The Foundling of the Forest		Sat., March 6
Turn Out		
The Apostate	Richard Sheil	Mon., March 8
No Song, No Supper		
A Cure for the Heart Ache		Wed., March 10
The Hunter of the Alps		
The Stranger		Sat., March 13
The Miller and His Men		
The Apostate		Tues., March 16
The Old Maid		
Pizarro		Thurs., March 18
The Old Maid		
The West Indian		Sat., March 20
The Hunter of the Alps		
Richard III		Sat., March 27
St. Patrick's Day		
The Gamester		Thurs., April 15
Tekeli		
Douglas		Sat., April 17
Tekeli		
The Belle's Stratagem	Cowley	Tues., May 4
The Turnpike Gate		
Laugh When You Can	Reynolds	Thurs., May 6
High Life below Stairs		
Alexander the Great	Lee	Wed., May 12
The Sleepwalker		
The Rivals		Sat., May 15
Love Laughs at Locksmiths		
The Road to Ruin		Tues., May 18
Ella Rosenberg		
Reconciliation		Sat., May 22
Richard III		Sat., May 29

The Purse
The School for Scandal   Tues., June 1
The Spoiled Child
Midas (burletta)   Kane O'Hara   Sat., June 5
The Jew   Thurs., June 10
The Liar

CINCINNATI THEATRE (*Columbia and Walnut streets*)
Douglas   Mon., June 21
Fortune's Frolic

LEXINGTON THEATRE

The Heir at Law   Fri., Sept. 3
The Adopted Child
Timour the Tartar   Lewis   Wed., Sept. 8

FRANKFORT THEATRE

The Heir at Law   Thurs., Dec. 30
Timour the Tartar

Index

Names of characters are not indexed, and titles of plays whose authors are known will be found under the authors' names. For a detailed list of performances, see pages 172-92.

Adams, Ann. *See* Usher, Mrs. Luke
Albany: Drake performs in, 132; Usher performs in, 97
Albany Theatre, 97, 111, 131
Allingham, John (playwright): *Fortune's Frolic*, 58, 68, 74, 150; *'Tis All a Farce*, 141, 144, 161; *The Weathercock*, 53, 55, 63, 67, 139, 145
amateur organizations and performers (unnamed): in Cincinnati, 68, 129; in Frankfort, 23; in Lexington, 3-4, 32, 33, 35-38, 48, 49, 81, 98; in Louisville, 23-24; in New Orleans, 129; in Quebec, 73; in St. Louis, 108; perform with Luke Usher, 30; permission to perform, 22
Anderson (actor), 99, 104, 105
Anderson, Mary (actress), 57
Annapolis, Blisset performs in, 103
Antony Street Theatre, New York, 97
Arch Street Theatre, Philadelphia, 147
architecture of theatres, 39-41
Argus of Western America, quoted, 150-51
Arnold, Samuel (playwright), *Man and Wife*, 93, 99, 125, 127, 135, 137, 153
As It Should Be (entertainment), 31
Atkinson, Joseph (playwright), *Tit for Tat*, 93
Auburn, N.Y., performance in, 113
audiences, 36, 66

Baille, Joanne (playwright), *De Montfort*, 82
Bainbridge (musician), 139
Barr, Robert, balloon ascent near lot of, 7
Barrett, George (actor), 99, 106
Barrett, Mrs. George (actress), 62, 97, 99-100, 104, 105, 106
Barry, Spranger (actor), 11

Barstow (owner of Frankfort theatre building), 78
The Battle of the Nile, 45
The Battle of Tippecanoe, 91
Beach, L. (playwright), *Jonathan Postfree*, 49
Beale (actor), 99, 104, 105
bearbaiting, 6-7
Beaumarchais, *The Barber of Seville*, 92
Beazley, Samuel (playwright), *The Boarding House*, 98
Beck (scenery designer), 25, 28
Beeler, John C. (owner of Louisville Theatre land), 151-52
Beeler, Samuel (owner of Louisville Theatre land), 151
Beethoven, Ludwig von, *Sinfonia con Minuetto*, 159
Behn, Mrs. Aphra (writer), 18, 143
Bernard, John (manager): appraises Caulfield's acting, 101; hires Cipriani, 52; hires Noble Luke Usher, 29-30n, 72; hires Mrs. Noble Luke Usher, 72; manages Albany Theatre, 97; manages Samuel Drake, Sr., 110, 111; refuses management of Lexington Theatre, 3
Bernhard, Duke of Saxe-Weimar Eisenach (writer), 137, 153
Betty (last name of child actor), 61
Bickerstaffe, Isaac (playwright): *Love in a Village*, 141; *The Padlock*, 9, 12-13, 23, 38, 43, 68, 87, 93; *The Romp*, 67, 79, 82, 89, 139; *The Spoiled Child*, 58, 60, 79, 82, 84, 92
Birch, Samuel (playwright), *The Adopted Child*, 87, 95, 157
The Black Forest (pantomime), 129
Bland, George (sometimes George Wilson; actor and singer), 85-86, 89, 92, 146
Blisset, Francis (actor), 62; biography,

This book has been set in
W. A. Dwiggins' Linotype Electra
with display set in ATF Caslon 540
and printed by the Printing Department
of the University of Kentucky.
Design by Charles E. Skaggs